What Parents and Teachers Are Saying:

"Your book is like a five-star restaurant with you as chef, serving up a meal with love as the appetizer, respect for our children the entree, and joy of parenting our just dessert."

—Catherine Bassos

"I've been testing your concepts and practices with my strong-willed seven-year-old daughter, and THEY WORK!
The resulting decrease in stress and increase in harmony around our house have been wonderful."

—Mary Smyth Seymour

"Your book was more valuable to me than any textbook I had in college. In fact, it's already making a profound difference in my classes."

—Eddie Cooperrider

"I appreciate the authenticity and vulnerability you show as a father who, like the rest of us, wants to be the very best parent you can be. Your message is impactful and powerful! Why? Because it's so personal and passionate. You are, without a doubt, a man with a mission."

—Marcia Jameson

"After twenty years of working with new parents, I thought there was little new I could learn. How wrong I was! Your book is like a light bulb dawning."

—Sally Piscotty

"The problems of the American family are outrunning the solutions. *The 10 Greatest Gifts* adds immensely to the dialogue. These are wise words from a wise man."

—Former Colorado Governor Richard Lamm, Director, University of Denver

"At last! A parenting program that fosters internal commitment and responsibility in a society that sorely needs them."

—U.S. Senator Hank Brown

"Read it. Read it again. There's something in all this or it wouldn't make you feel so good. Feelings are rooted pretty deep. They're not to be denied and they merit trust. Scientific analysis is not their reason for being. I wish I'd read it when my kids were small, but I'll focus forward. I can hardly wait for my grandkids to come and visit."

—Catherine Lazers Bauer, Essayist

"The 10 Greatest Gifts process is incredibly effective for creating healthy, functional adults, children, and families—and that goes a long way toward creating healthy, functional organizations."

—Curt Pendley, CEO, AMCI

THE 10 GREATEST GIFTS

I GIVE MY

CHILDREN

Parenting from the Heart

Steven W. Vannoy

A FIRESIDE BOOK Published by Simon & Schuster
New York London Toronto Sydney Tokyo Singapore

FIRESIDE
Rockefeller Center
1230 Avenue of the Americas
New York, New York 10020

First Fireside Edition 1994
Previously published by The Vannoy Group

FIRESIDE and colophon are registered trademarks
of Simon & Schuster Inc.

Designed by Bonni Leon

Manufactured in the United States of America

16   17   18   19   20

Library of Congress Cataloging-in-Publication Data
Vannoy, Steven W.
The ten greatest gifts I give my children : parenting from the heart /
Steven W. Vannoy.—1st Fireside ed.
          p.   cm.
"Previously published by the Vannoy Group"—T.p. verso.
1. Parenting—Psychological aspects.   2. Child rearing.
3. Parent and child.   I. Title.
II. Title: 10 greatest gifts I give my children.
HQ755.V35   1994
649'.1—dc20   94-28157
                    CIP
          ISBN: 0-671-50227-1

Acknowledgments

Allison St. Claire. This project is helping thousands of families and children today because of Allison's belief, wisdom, and extraordinary talent. I have never enjoyed working with anyone more than this outstanding editor, writer, teacher, and parent. As I write these words, I feel a growing excitement, not only for our rare trust, respect and friendship, but for a lifetime of deeper and deeper understanding, growth, love, and joy.

Donna Nott. Donna has helped me—and all of us—"remember the magic" with her exceptional portions of belief, wisdom, passion, and love. She is a friend for life, and a priceless deciding factor in the "10 Greatest Gifts" project.

Emmy Vannoy. My firstborn. Ten years ago she gave my life a dream and a purpose. Six years ago I lost that dream and gave up on myself. She never did, and her love brought me back. She is my master teacher and inspiration for this book.

Alison Vannoy. My secondborn; a walking gift of love and goodness. I wish I knew how to validate and love her as purely and as wonderfully as she validates and honors me. She's another of my master teachers and an inspiration for this book.

Laura Vannoy. My former wife. I got lucky and picked a loving, caring mother for our children. I'm very thankful for her constant outreach to rebuild our friendship.

Helen and Warren Vannoy, my Ma and Pa. I am blessed to have parents who are such exceptional role models of unconditional love, wisdom, integrity, responsibility, and goodness. I love them dearly and am enjoying our relationship more every day. This book is their gift to the world too—because of both my upbringing and also their vital support during the building of the 10 Greatest Gifts project.

Ben McDonald, Lucinda Dummer, Donna Carter, Carol DeJong, Dianne Borneman, Don Krug, Dr. David Hartenbach and all of the Aurora, Colorado, public school system, Mary Kouri, Karen Saunders, Kathy Post, Vicki Cooper, and Inge Fox-Jones. This project, and the families and children we are touching, are incalculably greater because of the belief, love, insights, support, advice, and wisdom given unselfishly by these dear friends.

Mrs. Kamlet and Mrs. Brogan, my children's kindergarten and first-grade teachers. Special thanks to Ed Oakley and Doug Krug, authors of *Enlighted Leadership*, for their extensive support and guidance on concepts included in Chapter One.

Al Lowman, my agent, who has an incredible knack for making magic happen. I'm thankful he has added his talents and enthusiasm to our project.

Fred Hills, editor extraordinaire, who trusted his instincts and has been willing to follow his heart to make a difference for children and families everywhere.

And, finally, to all the *parents, grandparents, and teachers* who have made such a vital difference in the lives of all our children.

Contents

Mission Statement

The 10 Greatest Gifts project is dedicated to taking the struggle out of parenting and putting the joy back in. Our goal is to help families create their own unique family vision along with a workable, proactive plan to nurture and fulfill that vision.

Note to Readers

In each chapter, you'll find I've highlighted a few thoughts that have been of extraordinary value to my family. I realize that the points that may be most significant to your individual situation may be quite different. I invite you to grab your highlighter pen and make this book work for you!

Want More Information?

For more information regarding the 10 Greatest Gifts project, see page 272.

We Love to Hear Your Stories

Nothing brightens our day quite so much as hearing what has worked for your family. With your permission, we like to share your experiences with other families around the country through our 10 Greatest Gifts newsletter or in future books. Please call us at 800-569-1877 or write to: P.O. Box 5301, Denver, CO 80217-5301.

Discussion and Reading Groups

If you'd like a free syllabus on how to use *The 10 Greatest Gifts I Give My Children* as a discussion book for your group, please send a self-addressed stamped envelope to: 10GG Discussion Group, P.O. Box 5301, Denver, CO 80217.

The 10 Greatest Gifts Advisory Board

Charles Bebeau

Mr. Bebeau is Director of Training at Avalon Institute in Boulder, Colorado, which offers graduate level Jungian counseling programs. He received his Ph.D. in Social Personality and Clinical Psychology from the University of Colorado and has 25 years experience in counseling and psychotherapy, focusing on relationship and family issues.

GeraLine Drew

Ms. Drew holds her M.A. in Rehabilitation Counseling from the University of Northern Colorado. She has been a police officer for 15 years in the Denver Police Department and also works as a certified Drug Abuse Resistance Education (DARE) teacher.

J. Thomas Maes

Mr. Maes received his M.A. in Secondary School Administration from the University of Northern Colorado. He has been an educator for over 30 years and currently serves as the Superintendent of Schools for Mapleton Public Schools in Colorado. He does special consulting work in prevention, control, and treatment of juvenile delinquency, as well as programs for minority and handicapped students.

Vern L. Martin

Mr. Martin has been an educator since 1965 and currently is principal of Iowa Elementary School in Aurora, Colorado. He received a Master of Education degree from the University of Nebraska and completed the K–12 Superintendent Program at the University of Colorado.

Tom Melton

Rev. Melton served on Young Life staff for 16 years at churches in both Colorado and California. He currently is the Senior Pastor at Greenwood Community Church in Denver, Colorado. He holds his M.A. in Youth Ministry and his Master of Divinity Studies from Fuller Theological Seminary where he currently is working on his Doctor of

Ministry degree.

Sally Piscotty

Ms. Piscotty, RN, BSN, is Administrative Director for Women's Care, a division of the St. Joseph Healthcare System in Albuquerque, New Mexico. A graduate of D'Youville College, she has 21 years experience in women's health and corporate wellness and health promotion.

Bob Tank, Jr.

Mr. Tank is Manager of Coors Counseling Services for the Adolph Coors Companies. He holds an M.A. in Social Work from the University of Nebraska and has over 20 years experience in developing and managing mental health programs.

Dr. Adele Thomas

Dr. Thomas received her MBBS degree from the University of Western Australia. She has 20 years experience as a general practice physician in Australia, with additional work as a psychotherapist and parenting training facilitator in the United States.

Wanda Torbert

Ms. Torbert holds an M.A. in Education, Guidance, and Counseling from the University of Georgia. She is Program Director of the Georgia Council on Child Abuse, providing services on positive parenting to a 45-county region.

To the children of the world,
our purpose and our promise.

No Band-Aids, Please

Recently, many American leaders have helped raise our collective awareness that our families and organizations are in so much trouble. One after another, they've pointed out that, as a society, we seem to have lost our core values, that we've lost at least two generations of our children to drugs, crime, violence, inappropriate sex, and other contemporary horrors.

In this book, I'm not going to spend any more time focusing on the problems or lamenting the decline of our families and society. This is a book about proven, grass-roots, doable, proactive solutions to nurture core qualities and values in our current and future generations.

We all have wonderful dreams for our families when we first see our children, whether they are born to us, chosen for adoption, or blended in through new relationships. But all too often the real world starts to get in the way as jobs, bills, schedules, to-do lists, fears, and broken promises obliterate our vision of those dreams.

The "10 Greatest Gifts" process provides a way to rediscover and realize those dreams again—but with a much different twist. If we simply do more of the same old things in the same old ways we just get more of the same old stuff, including lost or broken hopes and dreams. This book is not about creating Band-Aids for old problems. Instead, it focuses on the ways you can immediately begin to achieve your vision for your family or school or neighborhood—for today, tomorrow, and the next century.

A teacher and counselor who participated in a "10 Greatest Gifts" seminar commented that her school district had recently mandated that the teachers nurture a core set of qualities and values in the children. But no one had ever taught them how to do that. "Now, at last," she exclaimed, "I am excited and committed to that outcome, because now that I've learned about these concepts and tools, I know how to do it."

This book is my gift to parents, teachers, grandparents, and all concerned leaders who want to move forward with their vision of wholesome, thriving children in a growing, productive society.

"I thought my job as a parent was simply to 'fix' things: to solve my kids' problems or the problems they were creating, to keep them off my back and under control."

". . . even without money, I could give them gifts that would transform their lives, gifts that would help them create a life infinitely richer and fuller than money ever could."

King Dad, Queen Mom

"Yuppie" used to be my middle name. I came from a tiny Nebraska farm to the big city and made it big myself. I ran a thriving talent agency. I hobnobbed with the rich and famous. I was surrounded by beautiful people. I had a beautiful home and all the toys of a golden boy's success. I was young and healthy and happy. Or so I thought.

I also had a lovely wife and two adorable daughters. At least I thought I did. But I was so consumed by being a big success that my family ranked somewhere around ninth on my list of ten important things to do each day. Since it was usually impossible to get past item five, my family eventually became the other people who happened to live at the same place where I went to sleep each night.

When my children actually intruded into my life, I used my old tried-and-true methods of parenting, which usually consisted of "Sit down, shut up, listen to me, do this and do that, because I say so." I thought my job as a parent was simply to "fix" things: to solve my kids' problems or the problems they were creating, to keep them off my back and under control. It was a constant battle of wits to make sure that they knew I was "King Dad"—and that King Dad always wins.

It didn't take long to learn the consequences of a life with these priorities. My wife and kids left me. I never thought that could happen to me, the golden boy. I got so stressed and depressed I started making bad business decisions. My business became so overextended I had to declare both personal and corporate bankruptcy.

I had lost everything.

A friend took pity and offered to let me sleep in the basement of a house he owned. Night after night in that dark, windowless, filthy basement I wondered why everything had gone so wrong. Day after day I dragged myself off the mattress, overwhelmed with helplessness and hopelessness. The days ticked by in a series of meaningless hours until I could reach unconsciousness again that night.

My self-esteem plummeted. I realized my self-worth had only come from externals like having my name on that company door or being surrounded by beautiful people. I had never learned to validate myself internally; I could only define myself by what my parents or my staff or the press thought of me. I wouldn't go anywhere because I felt like a complete failure, a nobody. For months I could not even introduce myself using my last name.

I was desperate for any expression of human contact, but I also felt I couldn't risk any kind of involvement. I desperately needed love while at the same time I fervently rejected it. It was a bitter, hopeless trap.

I began to contemplate suicide.

One night in a drunken stupor, I realized I had nowhere to turn but I was too scared to end my life and too afraid to go

"Whenever I interact with my children, either I can
just get the job done and perhaps leave them with
inappropriate qualities and values, or I can get
the job done and leave them with priceless gifts
of qualities and values."

"Please remember that your commitment now is
toward nurturing internal qualities and values,
and that takes a lot longer than
simply demanding that the trash
be taken out this minute."

forward. I was paralyzed—but staying where I was was pure hell.

I learned one of the most important lessons of my life that night. I understood a connection I'd never even contemplated before: the qualities and values my parents had given me, like integrity, the work ethic, creativity, and problem solving, were what had created the successes in my life. Those qualities I hadn't gotten—like self-validation or knowing my feelings—were what had me lying on this miserable mattress.

I thought about other people I knew. I realized how powerfully the qualities, values, and principles they had learned—or missed—as children were defining their adult lives.

In that same moment I began to think about my little girls. In my race to get ahead I'd forgotten how much I loved them until I lost them; I had never acknowledged that they were truly the most important part of my life. I was a terrible dad. I was a horrible role model for them. And my former wife, who had a great deal of money, could afford to buy them anything they wanted. I couldn't even afford to take them to McDonald's for lunch.

The clear message I got that night was that, even without money, I could give my children gifts that would transform their lives, gifts that would help them create a life infinitely richer and fuller than money ever could. Presents like bikes or clothes or electronic games paled in comparison to the priceless foundation the gifts of qualities and values would provide, both now and in the future.

It was such a profound revelation for me to finally comprehend the connection between the qualities and values we give our children each and every day and the control and responsibility they need to shape and define their lives today and in the future. I knew that if my daughters didn't get these gifts as they were growing up they could end up in a miserable, painful, unfulfilling life. And I loved those little girls far too much to let that happen.

What would their lives be like without these gifts, especially years from now? And if their parents didn't give them these gifts, who would? I knew with absolute clarity that nothing on the planet was more important than the job of parenting. Any list of priorities I ever had from now on would always start with my family.

The next day dawned clear and bright. I had a purpose for my life! I stood tall now, rooted in my commitment to make a difference for my girls and the world they live in. As Marian Wright Edelman so eloquently describes children: "It is they who are God's presence, promise, and hope for humankind."

And little did I know that in giving these gifts to my family I would give an even bigger gift to myself. I had to learn to model and live these qualities in order to give them away—so in the process, I have given these gifts to myself as well.

I'm not a child psychologist nor a parenting expert with lengthy credentials. I am a parent who has experienced a quantum leap in my relationship with my children since I started coming from my heart, since I started taking the "high road" of conscious choice in this new paradigm of parenting. I know now that whenever I interact with my children, either I can just get the job done and perhaps leave them with inappropriate qualities and values, or I can get the job done and leave them with priceless gifts of qualities and values.

I've been overwhelmed with the incredible success and profound transformation that more and more parents are achieving with these concepts. They, too, are experiencing a new joy in parenting as they consciously choose the values and principles they want to nurture within their own families. I'll share dozens of their stories with you throughout this book.

A few of these stories may sound too good to be true. Every one is retold exactly as it happened or as the parents have related it to us in seminars or in follow-up sessions, letters, and phone calls. Does that mean that your results will always be this good or this immediate? Maybe not, because so much depends on the children's past experiences, other issues that are going on in their lives, who else is present in the room, or maybe even how firmly they've already erected their resistance to new ideas. These concepts often work on the first try, but remember to be patient with those who may need to experience your new mind-set and parenting style more frequently.

Also, please remember that your commitment now is toward nurturing internal qualities and values, and that takes a lot longer than simply demanding that the trash get taken out this minute.

Although the gifts you choose may be different for your individual family, in Chapters Seven through Fifteen, I'll share ten of the gifts I've chosen for my family, such as self-esteem, integrity, and feeling fully. In Chapters One through Five, I'll describe the five powerful parenting tools—focus, messages, teach, listen, and model—and how using them in the new way will shape and define your family today and in the years to come.

"I know of no more encouraging fact
than the unquestionable ability of man
to elevate his life by conscious endeavor."

—Henry David Thoreau

This poem was given to me by a dear friend some years ago. It's become a wonderful reminder to me of the vital job performed by parents and teachers and everyone who is concerned about children.

THE BRIDGE BUILDER

An old man going a lone highway,
Came, at the evening cold and gray,
To a chasm vast and deep and wide.
The old man crossed in the twilight dim,
The sullen stream had no fear for him;
But he turned when safe on the other side
And built a bridge to span the tide.

"Old man," said a fellow pilgrim near,
"You are wasting your strength with building here;
Your journey will end with the ending day,
You never again will pass this way;
You've crossed the chasm, deep and wide,
Why build this bridge at evening tide?"

The builder lifted his old gray head;
"Good friend, in the path I have come," he said,
"There followed after me today
A youth whose feet must pass this way.
This chasm that has been naught to me
To that fair-haired youth may a pitfall be;
He, too, must cross in the twilight dim;
Good friend, I am building this bridge for him!"

— Will Allen Dromgoole

Five Powerful Parenting Tools

If you have a photograph of your children handy, you might like to take it out now, or else picture them in your mind.

What are you feeling as you look at their picture or see them in your mind's eye?

Journey back to the first time you saw them. What did they look like? Recall their hair, their eyes, the feel of their little hands. What did they sound like? Were they moving or still? What did it feel like as they snuggled close to you?

If you have stepchildren, what are your memories of first meeting them, playing with them, cuddling them?

If you are a teacher, what was the first moment that a particular child captured your attention?

If you are a grandparent, when did you first hear about or see or hug your grandchild?

Can you experience again that unbridled love and adoration you felt? The pride, the joy, the hope?

I know that you have some gifts in mind you want desperately to give your children, such as high self-esteem, a sense of abundance, creativity, independence, integrity, and the ability to make healthy choices. Many of these gifts probably flashed through your mind as you gazed at your child for the first time with loving awe and wonder.

Many of those hopes undoubtedly surge up again when you're flushed with pride at your child's performance on the sports field or at a school play. But do you ever stop to think about these gifts of qualities and values when you're caught up in the midst of refereeing a hair-pulling sibling squabble or the endless struggle to get this child washed/dressed/fed/in bed or out the door on time? Or maybe it's getting the child's teeth brushed, room picked up, clothes put away, pets fed, trash taken out, or homework done? (Pick your favorite scenario.)

I intended to raise the finest children on the planet, just as my parents had. But despite my good intentions, I walked around in a fog, simply reacting to situations, never understanding that I had a choice in every reaction I had, every action I took. I never even realized that my choice of "reactions" to everyday occurrences gave my daughters the qualities and values that could either enhance or handicap their lives.

I firmly believed that parenting was about taking all the responsibility, making all the decisions, solving all the problems, always fixing and controlling everyone's behavior. It made the job of parenting feel like I was carrying around a backpack of bricks.

It never occurred to me that I had as much choice about what I put into my children's heads and hearts as I did about their physical surroundings. It also never occurred to me that by nurturing their heads and hearts with these gifts, a lot of the problems and behaviors I thought I needed to fix resolved themselves. I never realized that I could be proactive instead of reactive in my parenting.

It's relatively simple to babyproof your house, use a car safety seat, or teach the kids not to run heedlessly out into the street—we all do these things as a matter of course to head off problems before they come up. The important point is that you can make it as commonplace to be as proactive a parent in the mental and emotional parts of your children's lives as in the physical areas.

I think of this proactive mind-set as "new" parenting, a whole new paradigm or attitude of approaching each and every interaction you have with your family or any other child in your life. It's a way of seeing that you can choose a number of ways to approach any situation, but that some approaches will creep in on the "low road" and others will soar in on the "high road." Either road gets you to the same destination—that is, the room will get cleaned, the dishes washed, the homework done, the fight stopped. But the qualities and values and principles—the gifts you leave with your children as a result of each interaction—will be vastly different.

One brief moment in a grocery store clarified the concept for me. It was right before dinner time and I observed two tired, harried moms needing to get their shopping chore done as quickly as possible.

One mother was sorting through a pile of apples, choosing the ones she liked best. Her young son reached out from the child's seat in the grocery cart and picked up one he liked, to add to the sack. His mother's reaction? "Don't touch, I'll choose, that one doesn't look very good to me, stay still, don't argue with me. I'll spank you if you keep touching stuff." Her message from this low-road approach? "Don't be curious, I'm in charge, your opinion's not important, stifle your energy, don't think, I'm not interested in what you have to say. You're a bad kid."

Another mother just a few feet away was also looking at some produce. Her young daughter reached out from the cart to

"I intended to raise the finest children on
the planet, just as my parents had.
But despite my good intentions,
I walked around in a fog,
reacting to situations, never understanding
that I had a choice in every reaction I had,
every action I took.

"It never occurred to me that I had as much
choice about what I put into my children's
heads and hearts as I did about
their physical surroundings."

touch some broccoli. She was entranced by the vegetable's odd surface. She asked why it was like that. Her mother responded: "Do you have any ideas why it's so knobby? No? I don't either, but let's find out when we go to the library next time." This mom was definitely on the high road. Her messages were loud and clear: "I'm glad you're curious. I value your opinion and ideas. Think creatively. Let's figure out how to find an answer. You're a good kid."

They both went on to get their shopping done. Each mom had just spent less than 30 seconds adding to a pattern that would shape and define her child's life for years to come.

More and more parents are realizing they can choose either the high road or the low road to achieve the same basic result in the here and now. Before you even picked up this book, you probably already knew that your approach would have profound effects on how your children think about themselves, how they assess their ability to think, to decide, to act, to control their lives.

I suspect you already try to take the high road. You probably even find it's pretty easy—when you're having a good day. I'd like to share five simple tools to ensure that you take this road even when the world seems to be tumbling in on you, when the kids are snarling and the cat is throwing up, or when you're just plain tired and the job of parenting is just one more thing to get done.

Will using these tools mean you'll ride off into a glorious sunset of "happily ever after"? Unfortunately, no. These tools are not a cure-all. Stuff will still happen. Some days will still be the pits. But frequently the old ways don't work because we're still trying to solve the same problems over and over again.

The good news is that using these tools dramatically reduces episodes of acting up and acting out. Feedback from people who use these tools regularly reveals that the situations that do arise are handled much more quickly. They all describe important changes as they watch the children blossom from each experience.

The best stories come from the parents and teachers who have attended our "10 Greatest Gifts" seminars. Here are three situations which might sound familiar to you:

We went back to my folks' house for Christmas vacation last year in a brand new car. Nine-year-old Emmy was bored in a few miles and became fascinated by the little vanity mirror in the sun visor over her seat. She'd pull the visor down, flip up the mirror cover, flip it down, flip it up, down, shove the visor up and then start all over again. Endlessly.

I'd yell, "Emmy, stop playing with the visor. It could break." She'd stop. Five miles later she'd start again. More yelling. Five miles of quiet and down would come the visor again. I was definitely not willing to let this go on for 450 more miles.

Finally I realized I was lapsing back into all my old ways, giving my daughter crummy old messages and values, like "You're a bad girl, you're not responsible, you can't think for yourself." When I tried the "new" way, she stopped, thought about it, and the visor has never come down again since. Another brick out of my pack.

Hank and Nancy had an adorable little girl and a smooth family life—until little Miss Adorable reached puberty and all hell broke loose. The old methods, such as "Do you want to wear the red coat or the blue coat?" which had worked when she was younger, were no longer effective.

They stopped listening to her, she stopped listening to them. They yelled and lectured and cajoled. She went on and did whatever she wanted. Things finally boiled over when they laid down the law that she could only smoke out-

*side the house and couldn't leave cigarette butts lying
around. But guess what they had to clean off the lawn and
porch every day?*

These parents finally got sick and tired of hearing themselves say "If I've told you once, I've told you a thousand times"
over and over again. "Telling" certainly wasn't working, nor
were their attempts to control their daughter's behavior. After
using a combination of these tools the "new" way for several
months (which will be discussed at greater length later in the
book), they rediscovered the loving daughter they once knew.
Lots of bricks disappeared out of their backpack.

*Becky was almost certain her three-and-a-half-year-old
daughter Melissa was going to get her fired from work.
Every day she arrived completely stressed out and ready to
snap at all her employees, because each morning brought
such a monumental struggle to get Melissa ready for
preschool and out the door on time. Clearly this situation
was not getting solved, despite all the techniques she'd
learned at parenting classes.*

*Becky started using all five tools to deal with the situa-
tion. Even more important to her than dropping her backpack of bricks, she said, is the enormous benefit of the
qualities and values her little girl is receiving from Mom's
new approach.*

Each of these parents started to use these tools not only to
handle the behavior that was causing them so much grief but
also to be sure they left their child with the gifts they wanted to
nurture—self-esteem, the ability to think, a sense of responsibility, love, integrity, respect, independence, and more.

It suddenly seemed only natural to them to treat their children the way they would want to be treated themselves; there

"You can make it as commonplace to be as
proactive a parent in the mental and emotional
parts of your children's lives as in the physical
areas. . . . It's a way of seeing that you can
choose a number of ways to approach any
situation, but that some approaches
will creep in on the 'low road' and others
will soar in on the 'high road.'
Either road gets you to the same destination—
that is, the room will get cleaned, the dishes
washed, the homework done. But the qualities and
values and principles—the gifts you leave with
your children as a result of each interaction—will
be vastly different."

could be no better gifts for the people they loved most in this world. And they were amazed at the results they saw in their children's behavior and their families' growth. We'll share the outcome of their stories with you in later chapters.

Does focusing on a proactive approach such as this mean that we abandon firm guidelines for our family's behavior? Not at all. Here's Mary's story as just one example.

> *One time when my son David was in fourth grade, his class was going on a field trip to a Japanese restaurant. I had already sent money to school for his lunch, but he insisted that all the parents were giving their kids money to buy a souvenir too.*
>
> *I told him he'd have to use his allowance if he wanted a souvenir. The argument went on for days. I kept gritting my teeth because I really wanted to take the easy way out and just give in.*
>
> *He took a final run at me on the day of the trip. "I'll be the only one without a souvenir," he said. "It's not fair. You don't care about me, do you? You just don't care."*
>
> *I had to gather all my resources not to lash out at him or give him the money. "Remember," I said, "your allowance is for these kinds of things. I know you'll figure out a good solution." He stomped off muttering again how his parents didn't love him.*
>
> *That night he raved about how great the field trip was— and proudly showed me his souvenir! Turns out he had just not wanted to spend his own money on it. That event became a turning point in his learning that if you spend your money in one place, you can't spend it in another. He had learned how to budget.*

Mary chose to stay on the high road: While teaching her son how to handle his money she was giving him messages that he was a good person, that he could be responsible, that he was capable of making good decisions. It would have been so easy to lapse back into the old power struggles of "I'm Queen Mom and what I say goes, you're too dumb to handle money, I have to think for you, and you bother me." Both ways would have maintained firm guidelines but given vastly different messages and fostered qualities and values Mary did not want for her son.

These tools do not involve memorizing techniques for solving specific problems, nor are they a special exercise you do at 10 A.M. Saturday to nurture self-esteem, for example. These tools do not involve the repetition of rote phrases that can be misused to manipulate kids or confine them to thinking there are limited options to solving problems. They are something you do every day in every interaction that involves a commitment to always parent from the heart, to consciously choose over and again to stay on the "high road" and bring these priceless gifts to your children under all circumstances.

As one parent said, "These tools have brought our family from crisis to joy."

"Good character is more to be praised
than outstanding talent. Most talents are,
to some extent, a gift. Good character,
by contrast, is not given to us.
We have to build it piece by piece—
by thought, choice, courage
and determination."

—John Luther

CHAPTER ONE

Tool One: Forward Focus

Sometimes I wonder about certain drivers I see hurtling down the highway. Their driving seems very erratic. Then I pull alongside and notice that while they appeared to be looking straight ahead, they were actually driving by looking in the rearview mirror. Some are checking their hair, applying makeup, shaving—whatever—and some are just staring in the mirror for no apparent reason.

A lot of families I know, including my own for many years, steer their lives the way these drivers do their cars—by staring in the rearview mirror!

We only have a certain amount of energy, time, and potential to use each day. Of the 100 percent we have, only we can choose where to focus it. And while at times it may look as if we're moving forward, most of us are really aiming backward—back at all our accumulated problems, what didn't work, what went wrong, who else's fault it was, why we can't get where we want to go.

Meanwhile, the families that are really going forward look forward, with only a brief glance back now and then to gain perspective and remember what worked before so they can do more of it.

It reminds me of five-year-old Jeremy's question: "Mom," he asked in a restaurant one day, "what's history?" His mom, Diane, gave him a lengthy discourse, drawing on her extensive college education.

"I could see by his blank stare this was not getting through," Diane said. "I asked him where he had heard it used."

"The waitress over there just dropped a fork and said 'Well, that's history,' " he replied.

The waitress had the proper perspective. She could have focused on how clumsy she was, what a problem it was that she would have to get a clean fork, how it disrupted her work. That kind of thinking would have lowered her self-esteem and diminished her joy and energy, but she let it just go as "history." Instead of reinforcing the thought that this was going to be "another one of those days," she instead turned her attention to moving forward.

Can we actually choose how to focus our minds and energy so that we keep moving forward? Absolutely! Let's start with three simple principles of how our minds work.

First: We can only focus on one thing at a time. When someone thinks he's simultaneously watching television, reading a magazine and talking on the phone he's fooling himself. Research shows that he is actually switching his attention back and forth from one thing to another. Dentists have discovered how patients listening to music through headphones experience less discomfort because they're focusing on the music rather than what's going on in their mouth. We all know how easily a child can be distracted from an upset with a hug or a kiss or a toy because he or she can only focus on one thing at a time.

Second: We can't avoid a "don't." Imagine I'm standing in front of you right now and I suddenly hold up a sign that reads: "Don't look at my shoes." Where are your eyes going to go immediately? You guessed it! You might have tremendous willpower and be able to stop your eyes before they drift all the way down to my feet, but the urge will be mighty strong to catch a glimpse of my shoes. This is because our minds have to imagine doing something before we can tell ourselves to do it or not to do it.

It took me a long time to realize that when I told my daughter not to spill her milk, she had to visualize actually spilling her milk before she could understand my words. If I tell her not to hit her sister, guess what I've done? If you think I've just presented her with a prime target, you're absolutely right.

Third: We go toward what we focus on. Have you ever watched a pothole as you drove down the road and found that's exactly what you steered into? Or started watching the white line along the highway at night and found you were soon straddling it instead of driving in your lane? Horseback riders know a horse will go wherever its *rider* is looking.

I remember the last time I went hang gliding. As I soared off the mountain cliff, a huge, soft-looking meadow spread below me. Only one tree interrupted its vast emptiness. Just one tree. Only one tree. A fascinating tree. I couldn't get my mind off that tree. Guess where I landed?

Which child is likely to do better in a softball game — the one who's focusing on the ball or the one who's trying to remember where to put her feet or how to hold her arms or grip the bat?

These three factors describing how our minds work are so apparent now that I think back to how we used to struggle with my daughter Emmy's "shyness."

When Emmy was five, she was painfully shy. I intro-
duced her as my "shy child" and other people would com-
ment on how shy she was. Since we go toward what we
focus on, of course, all she did was become more shy. I'd
say, "Emmy, don't be shy," but since we can't avoid a
don't, guess which direction her shy quotient zoomed?

The difference in her was like night and day once I
learned to adjust my own focus as well as hers. If she said
"hello" to someone, no matter how timidly, I focused on her
greeting and complimented her on it. (This is a process we
work on in "10 Greatest Gifts" seminars called FAC—
Find, Acknowledge, Celebrate!) If she shook someone's
hand or looked them in the eye, I noticed that behavior and
gave her lots of positive messages about it.

In just a few months she became one of the most out-
going, sociable little girls I know. And many other people
know and enjoy her as well, since shyness no longer holds
her back.

Each of us has a 100 percent portion of personal and family
energy to use every day. Where we focus that energy makes or
breaks our day and takes us either several steps back into the
mess we're struggling to get out of or many steps forward to
where we want to go.

On the opposite page is an illustration listing the choices we
have every day on where to focus our attention and energy.

We make choices every day. We can focus on what's not
working (the left, back side) or we can focus on what's working.
Since we can only focus on one thing at a time and since we go
toward what we focus on, where would you rather focus? Most
people say "on what's working," but where do most people and
businesses usually direct their attention?

Would you rather focus on all the reasons you (or your family or your club or your company) can't get the outcome you

ENERGY CIRCLE

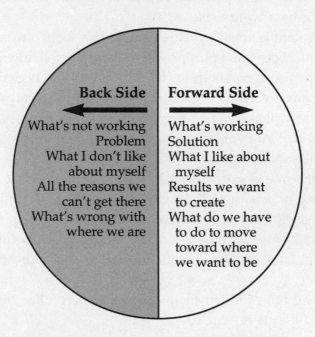

Back Side

What's not working
Problem
What I don't like
about myself
All the reasons we
can't get there
What's wrong with
where we are

Forward Side

What's working
Solution
What I like about
myself
Results we want
to create
What do we have
to do to move
toward where
we want to be

want, or would you rather head toward the results you want to create? Do you know someone who, when faced with a new idea or solution, can think of at least a dozen reasons why it won't work? I'll bet you know many because, sadly, that's the norm in our society.

When we're operating on the back side of the energy circle, we're stuck on the problem, on what's not working, on all the reasons we can't get where we want to be. We look for who else is to blame so we can justify why we're poor, helpless victims. Since we can only focus on one thing at a time, when we're on that side of the energy circle, we are indeed stuck there. Remember we can only be on one side or the other.

When we refocus our energy and move into the forward side, we concentrate on what's working, what the solution is, the results we want to create and what we can do to move toward where we want to be.

It's a simple reality of life—what you focus on is where you'll go. Focus on your problems, and they'll loom larger every day. Focus on solutions, and the problems begin to fade away. Focus on what uproar your household is always in and the uproar will get worse. Focus on the quiet moments when everyone and everything is functioning harmoniously and that peace will soon expand.

In the same vein, focus on all the reasons you can't achieve something or why it can't be done—and presto—you'll prove yourself right, or find more reasons than you thought imaginable. Focus on what you don't like about something or somebody and sure enough, you'll find more and more of those traits.

"I get it now," a woman at a recent session called out as we discussed the energy circle.

> I'm a mature, rational adult and a very careful driver. I've never had an accident, but suddenly I go through phases of dinging and denting the car. I realize now it's always after my dad visits from out of town. Whenever he visits he always insists that I scoot over to let him drive because, according to him, I'm not a good enough driver. When he leaves, I start running into things. I know now I go toward what I focus on. After a couple of weeks with him, I'm convinced I'm a lousy driver.

A husband and wife said at another seminar, "We're changing from having a 'TV' room to a 'family' room since we know we'll get what we focus on."

Families can easily find themselves hopelessly mired in the "backward" part of the circle when they gather at the dinner table each night.

My colleague Allison, for example, grew up in a very verbal family, all lawyers and teachers and writers. But there was also a predominantly negative focus of "Can you top this?" to their dinner conversations. Her brother's lousy day in school could be topped by mom's crummy day at home only to be bested by dad's horrible day in court.

> *We learned to score points by having the worst anecdotes. Unfortunately this translated into some pretty dismal responses when people would ask me, as an adult, how things were going.*
>
> *Unlike those reticent Minnesotans Garrison Keillor describes so well, I wouldn't even say, "OK, could be better." or "So-so, can't complain." Instead, I had learned how to make sure the inquirer knew my life was going much worse than his was. He'd get the full story on why I was too tired, too overworked, too underpaid . . . whatever was my lousiest item of the day. It's pretty scary to think what kind of life most people must have imagined I led.*
>
> *And, of course, I believed all that too. We go toward what we focus on! What a disgusting bunch of barriers I had erected to really enjoying my life!*

Imagine how your children will grow up if you ask questions like these at the dinner table or when you talk to them on the phone:

- What was the best thing that happened to you today?
- What did you do better today than you've ever done before?
- What did you do today that let you know how special you are?

"It's a simple reality of life—what you focus on is
where you'll go. Focus on your problems,
and they'll loom larger every day.
Focus on solutions, and the problems
begin to fade away."

"How can any child grow up whole whose
feelings are constantly discounted?
How does a child develop a sense of self if
he or she must conform only to what is
'acceptable' to the person or situation
his or her family tiptoes around?"

"Children simply tune out and ultimately
turn off when they are not allowed
to own their own feelings."

- Of all the things we do together as a family, what do you like best?

(Other examples of forward focus questions appear at the end of this chapter.)

You notice these questions require something more than a simple "yes'"or "no" answer, and keep people's energy moving forward rather than backward where they're stuck on what's not working.

Does this mean we ignore the crappy stuff that happens to our family or that we try to maintain an artificially "positive" attitude? Absolutely not! There are many times when we do have upsetting feelings like sadness, or anger, or fear, or disappointment. These are normal, not bad. The only "bad" feelings are those that are stuffed away or ignored. Forward focus is about managing energy, but there's no energy to manage, nor any way to manage it, if our feelings are in the way.

Denying feelings is what creates dysfunctional families. How can any child grow up whole whose feelings are constantly discounted? How does a child develop a sense of self if he or she must conform only to what is "acceptable" to the person or situation his or her family tiptoes around?

Children simply tune out and ultimately turn off when they are not allowed to own their own feelings. A close friend of mine did just that, resulting in lots of pain and expensive therapy as an adult.

> *In my house it was my dad's way or no way. I'd hear, "How can you be hungry?" when I knew my tummy was rumbling. Or, "Eat now or not at all," when I wasn't the least bit hungry.*
>
> *And that was just the simple stuff. Everything I liked or didn't like, wanted or didn't want, enjoyed or hated was questioned. "How could you possibly like that?" I'd hear. I*

didn't know how, but I knew I liked it. At least I did for a while. Soon I simply stopped feeling because not one emotion I had was acknowledged or validated.

We certainly will not agree with everything our children feel, but it is crucially important that we honor whatever feelings they have. That gift alone could be one of our biggest contributions to their lives.

I'm keenly aware that there are times when our circumstances seem too overwhelming to deal with on our own. Divorce, financial problems, job loss, poor health—so many situations in our lives can drag us over into the back side of the energy circle and keep us stuck there. In such situations, you cannot always expect to overcome these obstacles alone. Seek help and counseling from your church or a therapist if you feel overwhelmed.

But even in the midst of intense personal pain, managing your focus can be an extremely beneficial tool for you and your family. Allison continues her story.

I enjoyed 16 years of a growing, successful career as editor of a local newspaper. Then the company was sold, and suddenly, like so many thousands of other people in recent years, my job was eliminated, literally overnight. I was asked to clear out my desk and be gone in two days.

Sixteen years of professional life erased in a mere 48 hours! There was no farewell party, not even an opportunity to say goodbye to all those wonderful people who had played such a big part in my life. There was no closure, no finale, just watching my professional life dribbling out in ugly little tasks of sorting and packing, trying to leave some continuity behind for my colleagues.

After my intense anger subsided, an equally intense de-

pression consumed me. I was paralyzed with fear: I was single, middle-aged, had a son in college, and no prospects in a nearly impenetrable job market. People who were accustomed to hearing me describe what a backward-focused life I led before certainly didn't want to talk to me now.

I thought there would be no end to the helplessness and hopelessness that engulfed my life. I had adverse physical reactions to every antidepressant the doctor prescribed, so I couldn't even rely on medication for relief. I was convinced I was in a tunnel where the only light would not be at the other end but from an oncoming locomotive.

Life slogged on for months, pretty much flat line by now. No real ups or downs, no joy, no pain. But I started to notice a difference when I began working with the "10 Greatest Gifts" material. No matter how determined I was to stay stuck in my misery, I'd find myself focused forward after a phone call or meeting with Steve Vannoy. I was fired up to get the next project started or do the next piece of research. I was getting things done! I was actually looking forward to something!

While I was far from complete in resolving my depression, I had certainly found a new road to take toward overcoming it. I got it! I could only focus on one thing at a time and if that thing was how lousy I felt, or how depressed I was, or how many bills were piling up, that's what I got— lousier, more depressed and larger and larger stacks of bills.

When I started focusing on solutions, on where I needed to go, on the results I wanted to create, that's the direction I went. Amazing!

Another mother told me during a seminar one day that she felt like posting a sign at their house that read "RIP"—like those in graveyards.

All that time we've spent going backward is just gone, lost. May it rest in peace.

We looked and acted like a regular family. We both had good jobs, a nice house and car. The kids were doing well in school and were well behaved. We attended all our children's school functions and spent a lot of time with our kids.

But I realize now what an expert I was in pointing out what was wrong with my husband, the kids, the neighbors, and what I didn't like about myself. I was playing the game of life backwards. All that time and missed opportunities can never be regained. What's particularly painful is realizing that not only was I throwing my own life away but my family's as well.

It always surprises me how quickly children respond to the gift of forward focus and how dramatically it can change their day.

My seven-year-old daughter Alison was morose as we rode up the ski lift one sunny Saturday. She'd just made a run down the slope that was nearly a disaster, full of bumps and falls and awkwardness. She was down on herself and so, of course, her skiing got worse and worse. I was being a good "old" dad, making notes on all the things she was doing wrong, which would ensure she'd still be focusing on those things and doing more of them. I could have given her a whole lot of "don'ts": don't lean that way, don't use your inside ski like that, and of course, she wouldn't be able to avoid doing them.

Instead, I simply reminded her: "Do you remember what you were doing a couple of months ago when the ski instructor said you were the best student in the class?" Her next run was magnificent as she focused on what worked and how to do more of it.

Think for a moment about the cost and benefit of this simple change in approach to the situation. By pointing out everything she was doing wrong, that is, taking the "low road," the messages she was receiving were that she was dumb, she was awkward, she was a terrible skier. By taking the high road and focusing her toward her strengths, she learned that she was OK, she could do what she wanted, she was in control of her body, she could be a terrific skier.

An episode a young couple shared during one of our seminars probably sums up this concept best. They were visiting their priest for some premarital counseling. As the priest came into his office he asked them if they had noticed the beautiful Oriental rug in the vestibule. They had, and indeed thought it was outstanding.

"Did you also notice the spot in the corner?" the priest asked.

They hadn't. "Well," the priest said, "I know that spot is there and I always see it when I look at that rug. If you want your marriage to work, remember to always look for the beauty and not the spot. Whether it be a spouse, a child, a neighbor, a boss or a friend, you can find as many spots as you want to look for."

I understand now how much I always looked for my ex-wife's "spots." I looked for all the things I didn't like about her, and that's all I could see. The cost of such focus was losing both her and my children. These days my friends think I must have been married to a different person when they ask how she's doing. It's only because I now look for her "beauty," and that's what I find more and more of.

Unfortunately, there is no magic pill to clear up the undesirable situations that will still happen in our lives. But whether you're living through good times or difficult ones, where you

"If you want your marriage to work,
remember to always look for the beauty
and not the spot. Whether it be a spouse,
a child, a neighbor, a boss, or a friend,
you can find as many spots
as you want to look for."

"A common myth in our society is that
conflict is bad. But conflict can be a primary
motivator and an indicator of change.
Solving conflict doesn't have to be
only a win-lose situation."

focus your energy can make all the difference in determining whether you're having a good day or not. In fact, I can still easily slip back into making a good day a bad one just by shifting focus.

The point isn't really about whether it's a "good" day or a "bad" day. I've had days that were 90 percent good and only 10 percent bad, but I've focused on the 10 percent bad and made them into pretty lousy days. On the other hand, I've had days that were 90 percent bad, but I've had the presence of mind to focus on the 10 percent good and turned them into acceptable, productive days.

Focus can make such a big difference. Here's a good equation to remember:

AN EVENT + YOUR REACTION = OUTCOME

Remember the two moms in the grocery store I described earlier? The same event occurred—both children reached out to touch some produce. The moms' individual, and very different, reactions to the same event produced entirely different outcomes as to how each child experienced the event. You always have the choice of how to react, of whether to take the high road or the low road in your approach to handling a situation.

A common myth in our society is that conflict is bad. But conflict can be a primary motivator and an indicator of change. Solving conflict doesn't have to be only a win-lose situation. If we're stuck on the back side of the energy circle, we'll be defensive and protective, and conflict will become a power struggle. On the front side of the energy circle, you can approach conflict from a different perspective—find out what's already working and how to make the situation better for both parties.

One mom, for example, was constantly frustrated at her 15-

month-old Tyler. "My older son, Ryan, never threw food or did other annoying things like Tyler did," she said. "But making the list of special gifts we want to give each child helped me focus on Tyler's independence and gregarious personality as strengths rather than weaknesses."

Forward focus questions are one of the best ways I know to keep myself and my family on the forward side of the circle.

> *My little Ali was wretched with the flu one night. I couldn't do much but hold her head while she threw up. Afterward, when I put her to bed, I could see she was going to lie there for a long time thinking about how miserable she felt. She'd had a rotten day. Nobody had wanted to play with her and she was emotionally at the bottom of the pile. Her emotional pain was as strong as her physical pain and helped keep her stuck.*
>
> *I acknowledged her feelings by asking, "Honey, you're feeling pretty yukky, aren't you?" Then I spent a few minutes asking her things like: "What are some of the things you like best about me?" "What do you like best about yourself?" "What are you looking forward to tomorrow?" She was asleep with a smile on her face in just a few minutes. She could only focus on one thing at a time and that could either be how dreadful she felt or some good things in her life. And since she'd go toward what she was focusing on . . . well, you get the picture.*
>
> *I know that little girl well enough to know that without that shift in focus she would have tossed and turned a long time trying to get to sleep. She probably would have still felt bad the next morning. And I was able to sleep soundly, knowing she was comfortable and content.*

And just as it worked for her, it works for me as well.

On the trip home from a vacation at Disneyland, I was fitfully trying to sleep in my coach seat. At 3 A.M., the train pulled to a stop right under the brightest street light I've ever seen. My first inclination was to be really ticked off: the light was so bright I'd never get back to sleep, and we would be stopped here for at least an hour.

I could have stayed stuck in that negative mode for a long time and erased all the things I'd enjoyed about the trip. Instead, I realized that the light hadn't bothered the girls, who were curled up fast asleep in their seats across the aisle. Because of the light I could see them clearly. I had the opportunity to enjoy one of those rare and precious times when we can unabashedly stare at our children and revel in our love for them.

The light was even bright enough for me to open my journal and jot down my feelings and memories about this trip. My simple choice to refocus allowed me to experience the love, tenderness, and closeness of my children that I would've otherwise missed.

More important, I noticed once again that this episode was a juncture that I had formerly ignored. I had finally begun to see that I always have a choice in what to see and how to react— and that knowledge alone has transformed my life. In this case, I chose joy. Before I would have wasted precious hours or even days being bitter or enraged or in fear.

The Greek philosopher Epictetus said it so well: "We are not troubled by things but by the opinion we have of things."

When I first started asking my daughter Emmy what was the best thing that had happened to her that day, she reacted like most kids, with that atrocious seven-letter word—"*Nothing!*" The next time I asked, she looked at me as though I were a little less alien. A few months later, I was delighted when I asked her, "Emmy, what's the best thing that happened to you today?" and she replied, "Daddy, the best thing that happened to me today was waking up this morning and knowing you were going to ask me that question."

Unfortunately, these kinds of questions are still foreign to our society. What do you think the response would be if we asked people what's the *worst* thing that happened today?

"Forward focus questions are my favorite," said Linda after doing a "10 Greatest Gifts" seminar.

> When I first started asking them, my nine-year-old Katie was pretty typical of most kids. "Don't know," she'd say, or "I don't have any favorite things." After hearing my husband Pete and her brother Zach participate, she realized she was being left out of a lot of good conversation. She's as enthusiastic as any of us now. Those kinds of questions have really enhanced our sharing time at the end of the day.

Forward focus questions work with every member of the family. One man called us after a seminar with this story.

> I went home that night and asked my wife, who'd worked that day, what was the best thing that had happened to her. She'd never been asked that question before so she had to really stop and think. Her "best thing" was a small, relatively unimportant incident. But far more significant was my asking that type of question. She felt important, listened to. We had the best talk in probably twenty-five years. That night marked a vast shift in the culture of our relationship.

Forward focus questions can work at any age. Two-year-old Michael, for example, was too young to respond to his mom Michalyn's question when she asked him what the most special thing was that happened that day. So she decided to tell him something special. "Guess what," she said. "Mommy loves you!" Now whenever she says "Guess what?" or "What's special?" he delights in answering, "Mommy loves me!"

It works at the other end of the age spectrum too. Here's one mother's story.

> *Focus is the most critical thing we do. I found this out when my daughters were already nearly grown, one age 20, the other 16. But it's never too late.*
>
> *My older daughter was having problems in her personal life. One day she had a big blowup with me for the umpteenth time, blaming me for everything wrong in her life. Everything was all my fault, she told me constantly, because of all the terrible mistakes I'd made as a parent.*
>
> *I'd bought into it every time. I felt guilty. But I never stopped to realize how many positive changes I'd made in my life. I took a look at the fact that I was not such a bad person. I was growing and improving, making major changes. I decided to shift my focus and stop listening to her negative comments.*
>
> *When we got together again after not speaking to each other for about six weeks, I let her know that I was not my past, that I was living in the now. I reminded her that I would not play the victim every time she had a problem. I welcomed her to join me in the here and now or stay in the past alone.*
>
> *Instantaneously our relationship shifted. She respects me now. I did the same thing with my younger daughter with the same results. Focusing on the past, on what went wrong, only keeps you stuck.*

Another family with a teenager quickly found out which focus works faster.

The 16-year-old had made special arrangements with her parents to stay out very late on a weeknight to attend a concert. The next morning she was having trouble getting up to go to school. "Get your rear end out of that bed!" her mom yelled and nagged. Her daughter burrowed further and further under the covers, ears closed.

Dad came in to read his version of the riot act when he remembered the Forward Focus tool. "Wow," he exclaimed, "2 A.M.! Must have been a great concert. What happened last night?" he asked. Her face came out from under the covers. She told him.

He asked her what else made it such a great night. She emerged to tell him more. He finally said, "I'll bet your friends can hardly wait to hear all that." He watched her zoom into the shower and get off to school in record time.

So much of parenting—and teaching—is just like what our top teachers and organizational leaders do. If you want to get great performance from someone, you don't point out where they're weak or what they did wrong. If you want them to do better, focus on their strengths, and they'll go harder and harder in that direction. You already know you try twice as hard to please someone who thanks you for a good job.

I was meeting with a principal one day who was complaining about an extraordinarily grouchy school bus driver whom parents, teachers, and kids all complained about. I asked the principal what she did when she received a complaint about the bus driver.

"We go right to him with the complaint so he can work on the problem," she said. Of course, all she was doing was accentuating and perpetuating the problem.

Instead, I suggested she ask the teachers and parents to start FACing (remember: find, acknowledge, celebrate) him whenever he did something acceptable. Maybe they could comment on how they appreciated his getting to their stop on time or that he seemed to care so much about the children's safety. I recommended that she start asking the children what good things that driver did that day and let him know what they said.

The driver still acts a lot like "Crankshaft" in the cartoon strip, the principal told me a few weeks later, but she said everyone can see he's changing bit by bit.

Remember, what we focus on is where we'll go. We can only focus on one thing at a time and we always have the choice of what that thing will be. Perhaps one of the greatest gifts I can give my children—and my friends—is a model of someone who doesn't waste 10 or 12 hours a day standing still or moving backward. I—and you—can be aware of where our energy is going and where we choose to focus it.

Unfortunately, most of us focus not on the good steps as our kids go down the path of life but on every problem they create when they step off the path. We step right in to point out their mistakes, to scold them, punish them, and make sure they know what they've done wrong.

We were talking about the path of life in a session one day when a chaplain commented, "You know, I just wish when I was raising my kids that I had made the path a little bit wider."

Another mother wondered if being overly protective created such a narrow path our kids couldn't possibly stay on it. She recalled two incidents with her children.

We were in Italy many years ago when my son Adam wanted to eat a sausage from a street vendor. I wouldn't let him get it and admonished him about how we didn't know where the food came from, how dirty it might be, what kind of preparation it had, and so on. Of course, dozens of people were sitting around eating food from that stand and none of

"If you want to get great performance from someone, you don't point out where they're weak or what they did wrong. If you want them to do better, focus on their strengths, and they'll go harder and harder in that direction."

"One of the biggest revelations for me was to understand that *I* was perpetuating my children's misbehavior. I was constantly focusing on their problems and trying to fix them."

"If what we don't want our children to do is what we've gotten them focused on, and they can only focus on one thing at a time, and they go toward what they focus on—what have we been teaching them all these years?"

them died on the spot or even looked as if they might get ill—but I had to berate him, making sure he knew he was a stupid kid and only I knew best.

Another time we were vacationing in Orlando. While visiting Sea World my daughter desperately wanted a souvenir dolphin toy. Except, she insisted on a white dolphin with a pink nose which I wouldn't let her buy. "You can't get a pink and white dolphin," I yelled over her loud sobs. "Dolphins are gray, not white. Why would you want to get such a stupid toy?"

Many years later I realized I had been the "stupid" one in that incident. I resolved then and there that when my daughter got married someday, no matter what it took, my special present for her would be a white dolphin with a pink nose.

One of the biggest revelations for me was to understand that *I* was perpetuating my children's misbehavior. I was constantly focusing on their problems and trying to fix them. For example, when their rooms were messy, I didn't tell them they were bad, I didn't outwardly label them as messy kids, or use stern consequences. I just told them constantly to clean up their room. The message they got was that they were messy kids, that they couldn't take care of themselves, and that I would own the responsibility for the problem.

I also used "no" or "don't" as a matter of course, almost every day, in almost every situation. I'd say, "Don't leave your clothes lying around, don't leave a mess in the bathroom, don't forget to clean your room this week," ad nauseam. As Shad Helmstetter notes in his book *What to Say When You Talk to Yourself* (Pocket Books, 1986), the average American child hears the word "No" or "Don't" over 148,000 times while growing up, compared with just a few thousand "Yes" messages.

If what we don't want our children to do is what we've gotten them focused on, and they can only focus on one thing at a time, and they go toward what they focus on—what have we been teaching them all these years?

But the good news is, those same factors that run our minds can create the good behavior and qualities and values you want to nurture in your children. Quite simply, if we notice our kids when they're misbehaving or being irresponsible, or we constantly say "Don't touch that" or "Don't be a bad boy," that's what we'll get more of. But if we notice and acknowledge when they're being responsible or behaving well, we'll get more of that.

Change doesn't necessarily happen overnight. I started with small things—acknowledging one doll that had been put away or one dress hung up. But the improvement mushroomed to the point where a messy room is no longer an issue.

However, just as our kids will begin tuning out all the "noes" and "don'ts" we have hurled at them, they will also begin tuning out praise if it's used too much. I don't want to be a zombie parent who never notices or says anything, but praise must be sincere, it must be for their highest good and not just for your benefit or to manipulate them. It must also be specific, and it shouldn't be overused.

How often and what you praise your children for will be different for every family. One couple, for example, said they praise their children every couple of weeks about how well they play together, which has worked well to cut down how often the children fight.

Of course, there are times when we must say "No." The even better news is that our children are much more likely to hear and obey that "No" if they haven't been overwhelmed by or become resistant to all the other, often meaningless "Noes" we've thrown at them.

I now realize I was responsible for creating a shy child. I was responsible for creating an irresponsible child, for creating kids who were having behavior problems. Children are not born knowing what is "responsible" or "irresponsible." In fact, they literally don't know which way to go until we reinforce one behavior or the other. If we notice and reinforce the inappropriate one, that's the way they'll go.

I watched a little tyke the other day at a friend's family gathering. After a brief afternoon rain shower, this toddler managed to find every single puddle around. He'd run toward it gleefully, wade right in and stomp around, splashing water and mud all over his shoes and pants. Some even made it up to his shirt and face.

This little boy also engaged in dozens of other behaviors in this short afternoon. He'd come over to get a bite to eat, play with a toy, touch his mom or dad, swing on the swings, get a drink of juice—you know, all that random and purposeful activity toddlers turn their energy into.

But what was the one thing this child heard about all afternoon? You're absolutely right! The puddles. Practically every grown-up there said, "Don't play in the puddles" (remember, we can't avoid a don't), or noticed him while he was in a puddle, or afterward commented on his dirty shoes and clothes and face (we go toward what we focus on). By the end of the afternoon this child was a star puddle-stomper because that's what he was noticed for. And where do you think he'll head first the next time it rains?

Not only are we often creating exactly the opposite behavior to that which we desire, but the effects of where we focus may be far greater than we want to bear. Here's one woman's poignant story.

I separated from my husband when our son was just two. My father, who lives out of town, visits frequently to spend time with his grandson. Dad was in town last week and I realized after attending the first session of the "10 Greatest

Gifts" seminar how my dad gets on my ten-year-old's case. He gives orders or constantly corrects him or tells him what to do. I listened with my "child's ear" all week and realized that all my son is hearing is "Do this, don't do that, do something else and be sure you do it this way."

It really hit me Sunday in church when it was time to kneel and pray. You'd think my father could finally leave the boy alone. But, no, Grandad was saying, "Kneel straight, don't lean on your mom, put your hands like this . . ." All those instructions when the child was simply trying to pray. My son and I went back to church that night while Grandad stayed home and I noticed my son praying ardently. I complimented him on it and asked why he was praying so intently.

"I'm praying that Grandad will go home soon," was his reply.

What are just some of the gifts we give with the Focus Tool? The list is endless, but some of the ones I think of immediately are:

- Optimism, as our children learn not to stay stuck on what's wrong or what can't be done and instead stay focused on what's working and what can be done.
- Problem solving, as they learn to look for solutions rather than focus on the problem.
- Self-esteem, as they focus on what's good about themselves.
- Lack of defensiveness, as they're not looking for who to blame or why they're a victim.
- And so much more, like risk-taking, creativity, and a joyful attitude. People who operate from the forward side of the energy circle are just plain fun to be around. What more could we ask than to have fun with our children instead of consid-

ering them one more brick in our backpack of everyday burdens?

What's the best thing that happened to you today? What are you looking forward to tomorrow? What is the beauty you've seen today in your family?

Here are some more forward focus questions for enhancing every day's value, focus, energy, and communication.

- What has been the highlight of your day?
- What was special about that person/event/situation?
- What were the best parts of the concert/movie, etc.?
- What was it about this that you admired or enjoyed?
- What do you like best about a teacher, a friend, etc.?
- What is the value of that trait?
- What would be the benefit of that action?
- What are two or three things you are most pleased about?
- What is most important/fun/interesting about this?
- What are you most looking forward to doing tomorrow, next week, on that trip?
- What do you like best about yourself?

(Some additional forward focus questions that combine the Focus Tool and Teach Tool appear on pages 104–106.)

"There is nothing either good or bad,
but thinking makes it so."

—William Shakespeare

CHAPTER TWO

Tool Two: Messages

One morning I was listening to a radio interview that woke me faster than any alarm ever could.

A presidential candidate had heard a young woman singing at a local fair and was so impressed with her talent that he asked her to sing the opening song at the national political convention later that month.

What rattled me was when the interviewer asked the girl, "How will you feel if you mess up and make a mistake in front of millions of viewers across the country?" Oh, no! What a dreadful thought to plant in that child's mind!

But the 12-year-old replied with confidence: "I don't think I will, but if I do, I'll still know I did the best I could."

What wonderful messages that child must have grown up with!

Contrast that with a young man I followed around the grocery store one day. He must have been about six and the little guy desperately wanted to help his mother. But no matter what he picked out, it was wrong. First, he ran down the cereal aisle and proudly brought a box of his family's favorite cereal to the grocery cart.

"That's the wrong size," his mother snapped. "Why don't you use your head? Don't you know we always get the biggest box? Let me do it." The same conversation with slight variations continued throughout the store. I'm not sure about the little boy, but I had a stomachache by the time I followed them to the register.

And the checkout stand offered a whole new opportunity for the mother to defeat and deflate her child with more negative messages. He apparently had some allowance money he wanted to spend on candy, which, of course, is a major decision for a tyke that age.

Although they had plenty of time until their turn to check out, the mother kept snarling at the child to hurry up and make up his mind. "We can't wait all day," she said. "It doesn't matter which one you choose. The sugar's going to rot your teeth anyhow. What's so hard about choosing anyway? You're just like your father, he can never make up his mind either."

What an example of the old, low-road style of parenting: the job gets done but the child is left with some pretty dreadful messages—including the fact that his father is as awful as the boy is. With messages like that, how could this child ever feel capable or competent?

Fortunately, the next time I went shopping at that store I got a chance to watch six-year-old Jason shop with his mom. She's an avid coupon shopper and started each foray through the grocery store by asking Jason if he'd like to take care of the coupon products. He was thrilled to tear off down each aisle to find the right items. He'd match the product pictured on the coupon with those on the shelves, make sure the sizes matched with the sizes the coupon was good for, and then race back triumphantly to his mom. She always had a good word for his find.

Grocery shopping for Jason was a treasure hunt that was so much fun he didn't even realize he was learning to read, do math—and become a good consumer. By the time he was eight, for example, he had learned to calculate whether the coupon price for an advertised product was a better deal than the regular price on a similar store brand item. And when it came time to choose a treat to spend allowance money on, his mother found it only fair to wait as patiently for him as he had waited for her while she pondered over which shampoo or vegetables or dog food to buy.

What were some of the messages Jason got? That he could be trusted to act appropriately on his own, he was responsible, he could think on his own and make good decisions, and that he was helpful.

There are really only two kinds of messages we can give our children—hurtful ones that belittle or diminish them, or love messages that reinforce their goodness, their talents, and their possibilities. We read all those frightening statistics about how many commercial messages our kids are bombarded with in a typical week, but the number of messages they get from their parents is probably a million times greater, with several million times more impact.

Our messages are not all verbal either. The crook of our eyebrow, a gesture of our hand, a smile, a frown—all speak volumes to our children. What's the message when our child runs up to us eager to share something special and we say, "Not now, sweetie"? But when we go up to them with something to say to them they can't say, "Not now, Daddy." Or as all the parents at a recent session realized they were doing, rifling through the mail before they even said "Hello" to their family?

Imagine the messages I used to give my little girls when

"There are really only two kinds of messages we
can give our children—hurtful ones
that belittle or diminish them, or love
messages that reinforce their goodness,
their talents, and their possibilities."

"If I don't want to hear it, I don't want to say it."

"When our children are very young we focus
on every little step they take.
When they get older we start to focus
on every little misstep they take."

"What a difference you can make if you
always treat your children
not as they might be at that moment
but as you know they can be."

they wanted to hug my leg and I shook them off like irritating burrs. I was just "too busy" to stop and acknowledge them. Or the times I thought I was being a model dad like when my daughter spilled her milk and I didn't yell at her for spilling it. But then I'd rush in as she was cleaning it up and say, "Here, I'll do that. You're missing some spots."

The axiom that "actions speak louder than words" is very clear to three-year-old Alexander, who is getting two very different messages about bedtime. His dad explains:

> *Alexander's difficult to get to bed. He has a lot of night-mares. His mom says: "It's time to go to bed. I'll read a book through one time and then you have to go to sleep." She leaves the room, and he stomps out right after her. She yells at him to get back in and go to sleep. She screams, he cries, and the cycle of anger continues.*
>
> *My method is to read to him, watch him get tired, then lie down with him. I think it's much more important to give him love messages than make him feel bad because he doesn't want to sleep. I stay with him until he falls asleep. Even if he's a bit spoiled, I'd much rather have him know he's loved than have him feel unloved. I'd rather have him fall asleep while I'm patting him rather than sucking his thumb after crying. The bottom line is he ends up going to sleep in about the same time but with vastly different feelings.*

Do you remember hearing these kinds of messages when you were growing up?

> *You're not going anywhere looking like that. You're crazy if you think you are. If you think you are, just try me. . . . You better change your tune pretty quick or you're out of here. . . . I mean it, is that understood? . . . You act as if*

the world owes you a living. . . . You got a chip on your shoulder? . . . I don't know what's wrong with you, I never saw a kid like you. . . . I wasn't like that. . . . What kind of example do you think you are for your brothers and sisters? . . . Sit up straight. . . . Would you like a spanking? If you'd like a spanking, just tell me now—let's get this thing over with. . . . I'm your father and as long as you live in my house you'll do as I say. . . . You think the rules don't apply to you—I'm here to tell you that they do. . . . Are you blind? Watch what you're doing. . . . Something better change and change fast. . . . You're driving your mother to an early grave. . . . This is a family vacation. You're going to have fun whether you like it or not. . . . Wipe that stupid smile off your face. . . . What do you think I'm made out of—money? . . . That's no excuse. If he jumped off a cliff would you jump off too? . . . You're grounded. I'm not going to put up with this for another minute. . . . Don't look at me that way. . . . Look at me when I talk to you. . . . Don't make me say this again. . . . Where did you ever find friends like that? . . . Because I say so, that's why! Or how about this doozy: Everybody shut up—I can't hear the TV!

How do you think our families might change if our children heard love messages like these instead?

Good job. . . . I really like the way you did that. . . . Honey, how do you think we should handle this? . . . Thanks for cleaning up that awful mess. . . . I love your skill at fixing the lawn mower. . . . Boy, you made a great choice of cereal for this week. . . . You look gorgeous today. . . . That's a really great haircut. . . . You have the most precious smile. . . . Your help makes me feel so good. . . . I am so glad you're part of this family. . . . Will you show me how you did that? . . . I'm so lucky to have you. . . . Your smile

lights up this room. . . . Your friend is really interesting. . . .
This grade card is even better than last time. . . . What did
you like best about that movie? . . . I'm so proud to hear from
others what a great job you do. . . . You really have a knack
with those tools. . . . Your voice is so cheerful. . . . What do
you think? . . . You are very special. . . . I love you!

One mom summed it up so well when she said: "If I don't want to hear it, I don't want to say it."

Remember, it's always your choice which way to approach any circumstance. You can either hurt your child when he spills his drink by reminding him what a clumsy oaf he is, or empower him by letting him learn to clean up the results of his action. You can berate your daughter when she steals some money from your dresser, or you can praise her for telling the truth about doing it and assure her that you trust her never to do it again.

A simple message becomes our children's truth and that truth becomes their self-esteem. And that self-esteem governs their entire lives, their satisfaction, their success and their joy.

One mother in Wyoming looked up thoughtfully from her notebook at this point in one of our seminars.

I realize so clearly now that two or three minutes with
my child that may have been unmemorable and insignifi-
cant to me could impact my child's entire life. On the other
hand, I'm not going to feel guilty that I've ruined my
child's life with some crummy messages in the past because
I'm committed to shifting into a new, high-road parent
today. That positive shift will have a far greater lasting
impact.

Simple commands can change from "Don't run, you'll fall and hurt yourself" to "Please be safe and walk"; "Stop fighting over that TV or I'll turn it off" to "How are you going to decide which show to watch? What will you do if you don't decide?"

We can kill their initiative by telling them that they've got the stupidest hairdo we've ever seen. Or we can ask them what image they're trying to project, how do they think their friends will react to it, what do they think their teachers might think of it?

Remember the story I started earlier about how my daughter Emmy was driving me to distraction flipping the visor up and down in our new car on a long trip? The Message Tool certainly wasn't working the old way when all I did was tell her over and over again to "stop it." We all know "telling" doesn't work. The unspoken messages were: "You're bad, you're irresponsible, you're disobedient, you never listen to what I say." And her behavior didn't change.

I finally woke up to the fact that I was stuck on the back side of the energy circle. I kept focusing on the problem and how annoying Emmy was. I kept giving her all kinds of "Don't" messages which just got her more and more focused on the visor.

Instead, I gave her an "I" message which is a type of love message. "I" messages simply state what you are feeling without putting the other person down or making them feel responsible for your feelings. "I" messages can't be argued about because they are your feelings and you are the only one responsible for choosing how you feel.

I told her, "Emmy, this is a brand new car. I've only had it for a couple of days. I really want to keep it nice and I'm afraid that the visor might break if it's flipped so much."

She put that visor up and it has never come down again. She made her own choice and acted on it. The situation was handled and she was left with several good messages: "I trust you, I know you're responsible, you're a good girl, and you can think of good solutions," were just some.

I went into a convenience store one night to find a long line of grumbling, unhappy customers. The clerk's spiked green hair, black and white makeup, and black fingernails did not inspire a great deal of respect and confidence in these middle-class suburban customers. He was acting more frustrated and hostile with each exchange.

The clerk was antagonistic, slow, unfriendly—and I was ready to get back at him by attacking him with a hostile remark for having to wait needlessly in line and getting poor service to boot. I wanted to get his name and his boss's name and be sure he was reported for his surly service. But, I thought, dealing with people from the old, low road doesn't just apply to our families.

Instead of complaining about my long wait in line and his confusion about how much gas I'd bought, I asked how his night was going. I acknowledged the complaints and degrading comments he'd had thrown at him. He began to soften. Then, I asked him what good stuff had happened, what he was looking forward to that night. He brightened visibly.

I stayed around to see him greet and serve the next few customers with a whole new energy. I smiled as I left the store. Not only did his mood shift, but I was able to enjoy the rest of the evening, too, without simmering for hours with my own lingering anger and hostility.

There are so many junctions in our lives where we can choose to react angrily or decide to shift our focus to move forward.

I was racing away from a seminar at a military base late one evening, intent on getting home to finish up some work and still get a few hours rest before a session the next day. I think my mind was probably already at home soaking in a

"Good job! I really like the way you did that."

"How do you think we should handle this?"

"Thanks for cleaning up that awful mess."

"Boy, you made a great choice of cereal this week."

"You have the most precious smile."

"Will you show me how you did that?"

"I'm so lucky to have you!"

"What do you think?"

"Your friend is really interesting."

"You are very special. . . . I love you!"

hot bath because I sped through the guard station with tires smoking.

I glimpsed the guard from the corner of my eye as he leaped out of the kiosk at my truck—hand firmly grasping the gun in his holster. I screeched to a very sudden stop at this sight. But I was gearing up to be completely ticked off that he dare suspect me of anything, resenting the few minutes I'd be delayed.

I was ready to blast him with my righteous indignation when I instead chose to see the situation differently. I thanked him for reminding me that I was driving unsafely. He went back to his quiet night and I went home to that hot bath, both of us in a far better frame of mind than we were initially headed for.

So many situations end up less happily, though, when we go back to our old parenting style. One 17-year-old who'd been living on her own with a couple of roommates suddenly needed a place to stay and wanted to live with her stepdad.

When she called him, he agreed to let her move back, all right, but first he put her through hell with a series of backward focused questions and hurt messages. He attacked her with questions like: "Why were you such a slob last time? Why would I want you back here? How can I ever trust you again? Why can't you take care of yourself—after all, you were so glad to get out of here last time?"

He continued to focus on all her problems and how irresponsible she was. He lectured and put her down constantly. Her mom later saw how it destroyed the girl's confidence in herself and in trying to solve her problems.

Another way he might have approached the conversation could have been to ask her forward focus questions like these: "What would you want from me if we share the house again? What do you expect from yourself? What can we do to make it work? How can we get more of what each of us wants?" These kinds of questions would have kept their energy moving forward by focusing on solutions rather than problems, on how to help rather than who to blame.

Such a conversation wouldn't have been a cure-all or a quick fix. These two had a long history of problems together. But certainly this would have been a better way to work on some of those problems. And the interaction definitely would have given a whole different set of qualities and values to the girl.

Linda, a school principal, found that all communication with her daughter had broken down by the time her daughter was a teenager. The girl dropped out of school and things were definitely rough between them.

Linda was doing a four-day training session with us and each day took the new ideas home. Day by day, she started noticing her daughter's good traits and started asking forward focus questions and using love messages.

> Linda said to her: "I know what I've been doing poorly all this time. I want to try again with some of the new things I've learned. I want to hear how you want me to treat you."
>
> My daughter's room was always a mess. I used to say, "Why don't you clean it up? What kind of a person are you? How irresponsible can you be?" Now, I bite my tongue whenever I notice clothes on the floor or an overflowing trash can. Instead, I acknowledge her feelings and her opinions. I ask, "What might be the value of cleaning up your room? How would it feel? What can I do to support you?" The change has been incredible.
>
> If I had had this workshop earlier and been exposed to the power of focus and using positive direction, I think it would have made a significant impact on my daughter's life and prevented her from being a high school dropout.

Fortunately, one mom managed to communicate an important message in time to a son she adopted at age 13.

Marilyn noticed her son spending incredible amounts of time in the bathroom. She didn't want to break his trust by snooping, but one day he had left the door open a crack. She saw him standing in front of the mirror combing and recombing his hair into a dozen different styles while repeating over and over to himself, "You're a cool dude."

When he finally emerged, Marilyn asked him what he had been doing, that she had noticed him trying a number of different styles on his hair.

The boy started to cry as he told her how much it hurt that no one ever noticed him or told him he was a cool dude. Marilyn was passionate about staying on the high road. She said to him, "I'm going to tell you every day what a cool dude I know you are."

"That," said Marilyn triumphantly, "was the beginning of a whole new relationship with that boy I might never have otherwise known."

Our young children's most intense effort is to please us. Remember those early days when they learned to crawl, to walk, to put the correct peg in the star-shaped hole, when they learned to use the toilet? The most professional cheerleading squad could not have done a better job than you in giving a love message by FACing (finding, acknowledging, and celebrating) a job well done.

When our children are very young we focus on every little step they take. When they get older we start to focus on every little misstep they take.

We focus on and reward each developmental stage—walking, riding a bike, playing a sport, but seem to forget every stage in life is developmental. We're learning new skills and attitudes and behaviors constantly until the day we die.

I wonder why we give up that cheerleading role as our children grow. We seem to think that they ought to know what to do—behave well, get good grades, get along with other kids—so why bother to congratulate them. Instead we hover around like vultures, waiting for them to take one misstep or make one small mistake so we can swoop down with condemnation and scorn.

There's only 100 percent of a child's behavior in any given day, so it only stands to reason that the more we give love messages to encourage their good behavior, the less time there is for unacceptable behavior.

And when our teenagers are exploring the limits of their own individuality and power, we can encourage them to do so in safe, healthy ways with empowering messages. We can always choose to focus on their "beauty," not on their "spot." Here's what one dad told us.

> *I always thought my job was to point out my kids' mistakes so they could fix them, not point out what they were doing right so they would do more of it. I wonder if children would ever grow up and thrive if we only pointed out their mistakes? I wonder how much more they would thrive if we made a continuous conscious effort to point out what they're doing right?*

You can enhance almost any quality you want in your children when you find it and FAC it with appropriate messages. Do you want them to have the gift of patience, responsibility, caring, love? What a difference you can make if you always treat your children not as they might be at that moment but as you know they can be.

As author Matthew Fox said so beautifully, "Unhealthy families remind each other of their failings; healthy families remind each other of their goodness."

My brother John and I were brought up the same way on the farm. But he did a couple of things in our early school days that got him labeled a "bad boy." From then on everyone noticed him when he was bad. Meanwhile, since I was labeled a "good boy," they noticed me being good. So I acted like a good boy, while he behaved like a bad boy. To this day, I still think we are very much alike, but our labels made a vast difference in our lives. I know that he is an exceptional person but I worry that he still thinks of himself differently and limits himself in what he thinks he can do.

Tom, a well-loved minister in a thriving suburban church, told the other participants in a "10 Greatest Gifts" session about the night two parents' different responses created vastly different paths for their children.

> Tom started to get into some trouble when he and his best friend were about 16. It was pretty typical teenage behavior—speeding, shoplifting, and so forth. However, one day they got caught and dragged down to the police station. Their parents were called to come bail them out.
>
> The two boys were sitting together in a room when their dads walked in. Tom's dad came over, hugged him, and said, "I love you. What happened? How can I help?"
>
> The other boy's father walked over to his son and, without speaking a word, slugged him so hard the boy flew off his chair and landed halfway across the room.
>
> Three years later, Tom was building a life for himself in college when he heard the news. His friend had been shot dead while attempting armed robbery.

Kids believe they are what they are labeled. The picture we create of our children becomes their life. I'm reminded of a fisherman I heard about. He was catching quite a few fish but he only kept the small ones and threw the bigger ones back in. A

passerby's curiosity was overwhelming. When she asked him
why he kept only the small fish and threw back the large ones,
he replied: "It's because I only have an itty, bitty frying pan at
home." How big is your child's "frying pan"?

Teachers also can make a profound difference in our children's
lives through love messages and how they see their students.

Linda and Pete's nine-year-old daughter Katie, for example,
had learning disabilities and multiple health problems. Never
much of an achiever in school, she jumped way ahead in reading when her teacher gave her an award for being a good
learner. It was a simple message with a far-reaching effect.

Another teacher told me during a seminar that she inadver-
tently gave a student an A for a semester grade when he usually
earned only D's and C's.

After that, he legitimately earned A's and B's.

Even more touching and powerful is the following story
about Teddy. (I wish I knew the source of this beautiful piece so
I could thank the author.) My own daughter Ali might have become a little "Teddy" except for the love and concern of a very
special teacher.

THREE LETTERS FROM TEDDY

Teddy's letter came today, and now that I've read it, I will place it in my cedar chest with the other things that are important to my life.

"I wanted you to be the first to know." I smiled as I read the words he had written and my heart swelled with a pride that I had no right to feel.

I have not seen Teddy Stallard since he was a student in my fifth grade class, 15 years ago. It was early in my career, and I had only been teaching for two years.

From the first day he stepped into my classroom, I disliked Teddy. Teachers (although everyone knows differently) are not supposed to have favorites in a class, but most especially are they not to show dislike for a child, any child.

Nevertheless, every year there are one or two children that one cannot help but become attached to, for teachers are human, and it is human nature to like bright, pretty, intelligent people, whether they are 10 years old or 25. And sometimes, not too often fortunately, there will be one or two students to whom the teacher just can't seem to relate.

I had thought myself quite capable of handling my personal feelings along that line until Teddy walked into my life. There wasn't a child I particularly liked that year, but Teddy was most assuredly one I disliked.

He was dirty. Not just occasionally, but all the time. His hair hung over his ears, and he actually had to hold it out of his eyes as he wrote his papers in class. (And this

was before it was fashionable to do so!) Too, he had a pe-
culiar odor about him which I could never identify. His
physical faults were many, and his intellect left a lot to
be desired, also. By the end of the first week, I knew he
was hopelessly behind the others. Not only was he behind; he was just plain slow! I began to withdraw from him
immediately.

Any teacher will tell you that it's more of a pleasure to
teach a bright child. It is definitely more rewarding for
one's ego. But any teacher worth her credentials can
channel work to the bright child, keeping him challenged
and learning, while she puts her major effort on the
slower ones. Any teacher can do this. Most teachers do
it, but I didn't, not that year. In fact, I concentrated on
my best students and let the others follow along as best
they could. Ashamed as I am to admit it, I took perverse
pleasure in using my red pen, and each time I came to
Teddy's papers, the cross marks (and there were many)
were always a little redder than necessary.

"Poor work!" I would write with a flourish.

While I did not actually ridicule the boy, my attitude
was obviously quite apparent to the class, for he quickly
became the class "goat," the outcast—the unlovable and
the unloved. He knew I didn't like him, but he didn't know
why. Nor did I know—then or now—why I felt such an intense dislike for him. All I know is that he was a little boy
no one cared about, and I made no effort on his behalf.

The days rolled by. We made it through the Fall Festival
and the Thanksgiving holidays, and I continued marking
happily with my red pen.

As Christmas holidays approached, I knew that Teddy

would never catch up in time to be promoted to the sixth grade level. He would be a repeater.

To justify myself, I went to his cumulative folder and from time to time looked it over. He had very low grades for the first four years, but not grade failure. How he had made it, I did not know. I closed my mind to the personal remarks.

First Grade: Teddy shows promise by work and attitude, but has a poor home situation.

Second Grade: Teddy could do better. Mother terminally ill. He receives little help at home.

Third Grade: Teddy is a pleasant boy. Helpful, but too serious. Slow learner. Mother passed away end of the year.

Fourth Grade: Very slow, but well behaved. Father shows little or no interest.

Well, they passed him four times. But he will certainly repeat fifth grade! Do him good! I said to myself.

And then the last day before the Christmas holidays arrived. Our little tree on the reading table sported paper and popcorn chains. Many gifts were heaped underneath waiting for the big moment.

Teachers always get several gifts at Christmas, but mine that year seemed bigger and more elaborate than ever. There was not a student who had not brought me one. Each unwrapping brought squeals of delight, and the proud giver would receive effusive thank-yous.

Teddy's gift wasn't the last one I picked up, in fact it was the middle of the pile. Its wrapping was a brown paper bag, and he had colored Christmas trees and red bells all over it. It was stuck together with masking tape.

"For Miss Thompson—From Teddy" it read.

The group was completely silent and for the first time I felt conspicuous, embarrassed because they all stood watching me unwrap that gift.

As I removed the last bit of masking tape, two items fell to my desk: a gaudy rhinestone bracelet with several stones missing and a small bottle of dime store cologne—half empty.

I could hear the snickers and whispers, and I wasn't sure I could look at Teddy. "Isn't it lovely?" I said, placing the bracelet on my wrist. "Teddy, would you help me fasten it?"

He smiled shyly as he fixed the clasp, and I held my wrist for all of them to admire. There were a few hesitant oohs and ahhs, but as I dabbed the cologne behind my ears, all the little girls lined up for a dab behind their ears.

I continued to open the gifts until I reached the bottom of the pile. We ate our refreshments and then the bell rang. The children filed out with shouts of "See you next year," and "Merry Christmas!" but Teddy waited at his desk.

When they had all left, he walked toward me, clutching his gift and books to his chest. "You smell just like Mom," he said softly. "Her bracelet looks real pretty on you too. I'm glad you liked it."

He left quickly. I locked the door, sat down at my desk and wept, resolving to make up to Teddy what I had deliberately deprived him of—a teacher who cared.

I stayed every afternoon with Teddy from the end of the Christmas holiday until the last day of school. Sometimes we worked together. Sometimes he worked alone while I drew up lesson plans or graded papers.

Slowly but surely he caught up with the rest of the class. Gradually there was a definite upward curve in his grades. He did not have to repeat the fifth grade. In fact, his final averages were among the highest in the class, and although I knew he would be moving out of state when school was out, I was not worried for him. Teddy had reached a level that would stand him in good stead the following year no matter where he went. He had enjoyed a good measure of success and as we were taught in our teacher training courses, SUCCESS BUILDS SUCCESS.

I did not hear from Teddy until seven years later, when his first letter appeared in my mailbox.

Dear Miss Thompson,
I just wanted you to be the first to know. I will be graduating second in my class next month.
Very truly yours,
Teddy Stallard

I sent him a card of congratulations and a small package, a pen and pencil gift set. I wondered what he would do after graduation.
Four years later, Teddy's second letter came.

Dear Miss Thompson,
I wanted you to be the first to know. I was just informed I'll be graduating first in my class. The University has not been easy, but I liked it.
Very truly yours,
Teddy Stallard

I sent him a good pair of sterling silver monogrammed cuff links and a card—so proud of you, I could burst.

And now, today—Teddy's last letter.

Dear Miss Thompson,

I wanted you to be the first to know. As of today, I am Theodore J. Stallard, M.D. How about that !!!???

I'm going to be married in July, the 22nd to be exact. I wanted to ask you if you would come and sit where Mom would sit if she were here. I will have no family there as Dad died last year.

Very truly yours,

Teddy Stallard

I am not sure what kind of card one sends to a doctor on completion of medical school and professional boards. Maybe I'll just wait and take a wedding gift, but my congratulations can't wait.

Dear Ted,

Congratulations! You made it and you did it yourself! In spite of those like me and because of us, this day has finally come for you.

God bless you. I'll be at that wedding with bells on!

Elizabeth Silance Baynard

CHAPTER THREE

Tool Three: Teach

How many times have you heard a variation of "If I've told you once, I've told you a thousand times . . ." come out of your mouth? Does the need to utter such a sentence ever make you wonder how effective telling your kids something actually is?

Have you ever calculated how much of what your parents or teachers or supervisors told you has simply disappeared from your memory bank? Or how much of it never even lodged in your brain in the first place? Or how often you've heard yourself say to your children, "Everything I tell you seems to go in one ear and out the other"?

How often have you instructed employees or co-workers on a new project and then thumped your head in disbelief when they came back five minutes later with a basic question on something you just told them? What makes some information stick and some float right by, you wonder. How could I present this material so they'll get it?

As parents, how many of you think one of your major tasks

is to teach your children? Aren't you full of vital information and wisdom and experience that it's essential they know? But just what is teaching all about? How do you do it most effectively? How do you make sure they'll get it, preferably the first time?

At this point I wish technology had already mastered interactive books so you could respond as you can with interactive television or on a computer bulletin board or at a live seminar. If you could answer me directly, I could do this entire chapter the way I have the first 225 words or so and never tell you a thing. But you'd learn a lot because all I'd do is ask you more and more questions.

We've already talked about the low road versus the high road approach to parenting, and the "old" and "new" way to use these simple tools. In fact, the "new" way of teaching is at least two thousand years old. The Greek philosopher Socrates knew that asking questions was the most effective way to teach so his students would get it. And retain it. The "old" way of teaching is what I see so many people doing today, which is to tell 'em . . . and tell 'em . . . and tell 'em some more—and then wonder why they didn't get it.

Not only do they not get it, what are the subtle messages they do get when we constantly tell our children or other people what to do? They're really hearing "I'm the boss, you're not as important, you can't think, I have to take all the responsibility here."

How long would you want to work for someone who was constantly telling you what to do? How long would you keep a friend like that? How much do you think your children are really listening when you simply tell, tell, tell?

Usually the first phone calls we get after doing a "10 Greatest Gifts" seminar are about this tool. Those calls start at about 7 in the morning the very next day with an excited voice on the other end saying something like, "How come I didn't know this before? Why didn't you say it was going to be this easy? I wish I'd known this years ago."

Do you notice how they've already learned to ask a lot of questions?

They're excited because, often, simply asking a few questions can clear up conflicts that have gone on for years. Getting three-year-old Ryan down for a nap, for example, had always been a major pain for his mom, Linda. She'd exhausted every possible reason that made sense to her about why he needed that nap. But after the seminar she simply asked him, "Ryan, why do you think it's important to take a nap?"

I can't remember what his answer was that made sense to him, but it was his answer, his reason, and he now settles in for a nap without a fuss.

The same held true for Wendy, whose seven-year-old son had perfected his resistance to washing up before going over to a friend's house.

> *Wendy trudged home from our seminar girding herself to face the usual hassle. Instead, when her son put up the usual stall and snarl tactics, she simply asked: "David, why do you think you should wash up before we go over to our friends' house?"*
>
> *His answer was something like "So they won't be grossed out and barf when they smell me"—not necessarily the same reason Wendy had, but again, it was his answer, his truth—and his resistance disappeared.*

It thrills us when calls pour in like this with resolution to issues from cleaning up rooms to brushing teeth to getting homework done. It works!

But, you say, my little girl's only two and a half. She doesn't know why it's important to brush her teeth. She's too little to figure out tooth decay and bacteria. Wonderful. That's a great time to ask some more questions like, "Do you know what Big Bird would say?" (Or your troll doll or Barney or Ariel or who-ever your child's favorite character is.) When the child says "yes," she's ready to listen to whatever information you give at that point. Then you can "tell" her lots of facts and know she's ready to listen. Salespeople know this as "an invitation to learn."

Earlier I said that although these tools work, sometimes they don't work right away. Yana shared an experience using the Teach Tool with her son after the first session of a seminar.

> *My young son had a friend over to play and was ab-solutely unwilling to share his toys. The whole afternoon was a major, very unpleasant battlefield. I asked him, "What's the value of sharing your toys with a friend?" Of course, he said, "No value." I asked, "How do you think your friend feels?" "I don't care," he shouted. The day went downhill from there.*
>
> *Later that night I asked him how he felt about the day. He admitted he'd had a terrible time with his friend. I asked him what he might do differently the next time, and he came up with a long list of things he wants to do differently. I didn't have to suggest a thing about how to be a good boy that he could resist. He knew all the best answers all by himself!*

We all have an intense desire to share what we know with our kids. We want desperately to help them avoid the pain and frustration of making the same mistakes we made. We can't possibly control the experiences our kids will come up against, but we can arm them in advance with the gifts that will see them through life's rough spots. The best way I've found to do that is through the high road of teaching by questioning, not telling.

One of the gifts I most consistently hear parents say they want for their children is the ability to make wise decisions, to think for themselves. Yet, if we tell our children what to do all the time, how can they ever learn to think for themselves?

At one of our sessions, a parent insisted that questions don't work. "We use them all the time," he said, "and they just don't work." Someone in the class asked what questions he asked. He said questions like: "Who did this? Did you do your homework yet? Why did you forget your lunch money?" The whole class responded immediately: "Of course they don't work. Those are backward focus questions."

These kinds of questions keep us solidly in the back side of the energy circle, destroying critical thinking, a sense of responsibility, confidence, and joy. Questions from the front side look at what's working, help weigh options, build decision making, creativity, solutions, confidence, and so much more.

Last summer my girls and I constructed a tree house in our back yard. I had to swallow hard to avoid shouting "No" immediately when my six-year-old wanted to use the circular saw to cut some of the wood. "Questions," I muttered to myself. "Practice what you teach. Ask questions."

I started with: "Ali, what do you need to know about this saw to use it carefully? What do you need to do to protect your eyes and hands? How would you use it on this board?" And so on. If there was an answer she didn't know or couldn't figure out, I'd ask if she wanted to know what I knew about it. Both girls did try to use the saw, but quickly realized through their own discovery it was dangerous. They themselves decided not to use it.

If I had simply told them it was dangerous and to stay away from it, where do you think they would have headed first?

We have an incredible tree house now, designed and mostly

"We can't possibly control the experiences
our kids will come up against, but we can arm
them in advance with the gifts
that will see them through life's rough spots."

"I consider the Teach Tool to be virtually
a life or death tool: Our children
actually learn to think for themselves,
and when we do have to tell them something
important, they won't tune us out."

built by two very creative, very careful little girls who learned an enormous amount about wood and tools and balance and design and construction. And I hardly told them a thing.

What's even more important are the qualities and values they incorporated from the experience. They learned to think creatively; this house was entirely their creation, not built from a packaged design. They learned that their ideas were valuable, and how to compromise and negotiate when ideas clashed. They learned how to accomplish a big task and how to stick with it until it was finished, even when the project got difficult. They learned how to learn, how to research information they were missing, how to acquire new skills. And, needless to say, their self-esteem quotient soared off the scale.

There's another benefit to this tool. When I used to tell, and tell, and tell my kids some more, they simply stopped listening to anything I had to say. When I had something really important to say, they still weren't listening. Now when I do have to tell them something, they are much more likely to be actually listening to what I have to say.

I consider the Teach Tool to be virtually a life or death tool: Our children actually learn to think for themselves, and when we do have to tell them something important, they won't tune us out. Here's what one couple related at a seminar follow-up.

We used to use time-outs all the time with our little boys. It was frustrating because time-outs just didn't work. Now we use questions. If our preschooler bites or hits the baby, for example, we ask, "What should we do about what just happened? How do you think the baby feels about what happened?" He'll answer something like, "I was angry at him," or "I don't like him." We listen, honor his feelings and then ask again what we should do about it, since hitting or biting is not an acceptable way to show anger.

The questions let him be part of the solution. When we were punitive with time-outs, he usually ended up madder than ever and repeated the behavior. Now he thinks of other things to do. After we ask him questions, he'll go over and comfort the baby and give him a hug—on his own and not because we suggested it.

We hear hundreds of stories from parents regarding homework, grades, and school. Here were the dramatic results when Donna switched from her "old" parenting style to the "new" way.

My son Brian was failing English even though he's always been an A or B student. I tried telling him and telling him how important it was for him to do well. I nagged him about his homework. I told him what to study and when to study it. Clearly none of this worked because his grades didn't improve one bit.

After I switched to using questions instead of telling, the problem evaporated. I asked him things like the following— and, of course, listening very closely to his answers, honoring his opinions and feelings, and giving him lots of love messages: "Do you still enjoy football a lot? What does it feel like when you do well on the field? What would it feel like if you did well in English? Do you want to use things you learned in football later on in life?" (At that time he thought maybe he'd like to be a sportscaster.) "Does English class teach you about communicating well? Do you think learning to be a better communicator would help you be a better sportscaster?"

And, finally, the most important question: "What can I do to assist you in getting what you want?"

Only a few months later I got a wonderful call at work. It was Brian letting me know he'd gotten a B in English!

All along, the answers were always his and because they were his, he owned them. They became his own motivation and internal commitment to doing what he wanted and needed to do. I could almost see his self-esteem and excitement for learning bloom before my eyes.

Another dad I know is still telling and telling his teenagers to do their chores around the house, and clearly "telling" is not working. He's had to escalate to such actions as threatening the boys with no supper until the dog is fed. He's also expending incredible amounts of energy arguing about washing the dishes. Last I heard he was actually putting the dirty dishes on the boys' beds, which the boys promptly transferred to the floor, where they got moldier with every passing day.

Are these "bad" boys? Not at all. I happen to see them frequently when they stay with their mom. They hop up after each meal, do their dishes and help clean up the kitchen without a word. Actually, there are several words but they are comments like: "Thanks so much for helping clean up. You do a great job with those dishes. Do you think the kitchen is as clean as we'd like it to be? What can I do to help?"

Feeding their pets isn't a problem either. She lets them decide what the important chores are by asking them, "What are the most important things to do to keep the dog healthy and happy? I like your choices. How should we divide the chores up?"

When she sees them completing a task, she FACs them and says: "It's so nice to see when you make a commitment that you follow through on it. You're great to have around."

Do they always do it perfectly? "Of course not!" their mother says. "Neither do I. But if I were to notice when they're not perfect and tell them, 'Be sure to take your dishes to the sink,' it would be giving them a picture of themselves as messy and irresponsible."

What an entirely different set of qualities and values these young men are getting from the two approaches not to mention the different messages they are getting, both spoken and unspoken.

I'll never forget one mother's stunned reaction following this segment of a "10 Greatest Gifts" seminar. While nearly everyone else left for a break, she sat in total, almost meditative silence. Finally, she said:

> *I am a language teacher. I speak three foreign languages and yet this is the most foreign—but without contest, the most important—one I've ever encountered. I've had more than 18 years of formal schooling and I read constantly, but I've never seen or heard of this before. I honestly never knew there was another way to communicate with children. How can I get this into my school's curriculum?*
>
> *I've been sitting here rerunning dozens of both pleasant and less-than-satisfactory situations in my mind—things that have happened recently with my students and my own children. I can't think of a single one that would not have been incredibly enhanced if I had just used this Teach Tool; if I had only asked questions instead of jumping right in with my own opinions and facts. I never knew there was an alternative to always having to tell everybody everything to think and do—especially if they're younger and shorter than I.*
>
> *I certainly do not ever want to discourage any child from learning Spanish or Japanese or Farsi or whatever they want, but I fervently hope their parents will first teach them Questions, the most special language of all.*

Debbie used forward focus questions to help her son and his friends work through what could have been an explosive situation at school. Because of a lot of gang activity at their school, it imposed a rigid new dress code that banned clothing favored by gang members.

> *My son is a super jock, a good football player, and a good student. But much of his clothing was the banned stuff. He came home all in a twist, angry and confused, convinced it wasn't fair. I know a lot of parents who helped stoke the students' agitation, which only aggravated the situation more.*
>
> *I agreed with him that the ban wasn't very fair, but I didn't want to stay on the back side of the energy circle focusing on the problem, figuring out who to blame, encouraging the kids to stay victims.*
>
> *Instead, I asked him things like: What did he think a gang member was and why would people not want them around? Why did he think the administration made this decision? Did he think they did it just to be punitive? I asked him if he wanted to hear what I'd learned about gangs. By asking questions and keeping communications going, I really think he felt a lot more comfortable and he shared a lot of his insights with his friends—which helped calm them down too.*

Another mom wrote us about taking her 17-year-old daughter out to shop for a prom dress.

> *Of course, my daughter aimed right for the most outrageous outfit she could find. I hated what she picked out; my father would have had an unprintable opinion about that dress, most of which would have revolved around red lights and scarlet women.*
>
> *I almost went into my old routine. But I realized telling her my opinion would only create resistance and that dress would surely have ended up going home with us. Instead, I started asking questions. "How do you want to come across*

"I'm convinced that of all the tools, teaching
through questioning is the only effective way
to deal with teenagers. And if you start using
questions while your children are young,
you'll have already built a firm basis
of dignity and respect with them."

"Being a parent leader means you can now spend
your time exercising meaningful discipline instead
of meaningless discipline. Meaningless
discipline means the control still keeps coming at
them, not through them. Meaningful discipline
defines the limits and behaviors you have deemed
acceptable for your family, but bestows the
children with all the gifts of qualities
and values they'll need to establish their own
internal commitments and controls."

"Leaders, whether in business or at home,
find people are willing to do ten times more
than we could ever tell them to do when they are
motivated and empowered to work from their own
ideas and their own internal commitment."

at the prom?" I asked. "What image do you want to pro-
ject?" I listened, gave her love messages, acknowledged her
feelings about herself and the way she dressed. Completely
on her own, she came to the conclusion that she wanted to
project something entirely different.
P.S. I love her choice of a prom dress!

I'm convinced that of all the tools, teaching through ques-tioning is the only effective way to deal with teenagers.

Controlling, telling, pointing out their mistakes and short-comings, limiting choices, and imposing consequences some-times work when kids are little because you can still dominate and manipulate them. I know this tool is not a cure-all but it's a sure bet that the other techniques we've used don't work.

And if you start using questions while your children are still young, you'll have already built a firm basis of dignity and respect with them. You'll have treated them the way you'd like to be treated, nurturing trust, strong self-esteem, and close rela-tionships.

As one mom said during a recent seminar, "Let's treat our children like the visiting dignitaries they are."

Have patience, however. Starting to ask your children ques-tions is "like speaking a foreign language." Your children will probably be suspicious at first. Many of them are numb from too much telling or being trapped by questions that are really accusations in disguise. They're going to wonder about you ac-tually wanting real information for a change, you truly wanting to know what they think and feel. But keep practicing. The change in your family will astound you. A list of some forward focus "teach" questions appears at the end of this chapter.

This tool—like all the others—is really a matter of leader-ship. Leadership is leadership whether those we lead are three feet tall or six feet tall.

One of the primary differences between leadership and

management is commitment versus compliance. Managing means giving orders, telling, having all the answers, and all the responsibility, being the autocratic King Boss. But when managers learn to use forward focus questions, they access their people's best ideas, they transfer ownership, they transfer responsibility. Perhaps most importantly, when people discover they have the answers and that they can be responsible, it greatly enhances their self-esteem and their desire to contribute and make a difference.

When I was growing up, it was the parent's job to have the answers and give the orders. Those kinds of parents didn't use leadership, they managed by being King Dad or Queen Mom. In our seminars, parents are flabbergasted that they can be true leaders instead of overbearing managers.

Typical management—whether at home or in business—doesn't allow people to think or to take responsibility; it doesn't nurture qualities and values that allow people to have a natural commitment to their work. Managers have to do the same job over and over again to get things done.

I've been doing leadership training with businesses for over 20 years. The core of our work is helping organizations develop a culture where they use questions to consciously look for what's working as a foundation for moving forward. When leaders perfect this discipline they discover that self-esteem rises and resistance to change diminishes. We believe that this discipline is one of the most vital ways leaders can leverage their time, multiply their effectiveness and productivity, and improve quality as well as profits. The "10 Greatest Gifts" approach is a proven way to apply true leadership concepts to families. In addition to all these other benefits, it means treating people with dignity and respect no matter what their age.

Being a parent leader means you can now spend your time exercising *meaningful* discipline instead of *meaningless* discipline. As a manager parent you find yourself having to tell the kids over and over again to get their rooms cleaned up or take the trash out or pick up their toys. They'll obey—if you're still bigger or stronger than they or constantly watching over them.

Meaningless discipline involves controlling and telling and punishing. It only reacts to the immediate problem. Meaningless discipline means the control still keeps coming *at* them, not *through* them.

Meaningless discipline often means endless struggles, satisfying the parents' need to express anger or to feel the false sense of security they might get from controlling the kids. It doesn't do a thing for the kids, though. It doesn't focus on the resulting qualities and values; it denies our children the opportunity to develop their own internal control. They grow up lacking the tools they need for internal discipline to deal with the many problems they'll encounter long after they leave the protection of our well-meaning rules. They're much more likely to react negatively to anything mom or dad say rather than to define their own core values as a positive action.

Meaningful discipline, on the other hand, defines the limits and behaviors you have deemed acceptable for your family, but bestows the children with all the gifts of qualities and values they'll need to establish their own internal commitments and controls. The difference is staggering.

Leaders, whether in business or at home, find people are willing to do ten times more than we could ever tell them to do when they are motivated and empowered to work from their own ideas and their own internal commitment. Our kids will flourish beyond our wildest expectations when we provide the leadership to develop their own commitment to be the best they can be—when in fact we "teach our children well."

Forward focus/teach questions can be used in a wide variety of situations. In all circumstances they focus on what people really think and really feel, on what's working, where we want to go, what we want more of and additional options and ideas. Just like the first batch of forward focus questions that appears on page 65, these are all open-ended and can't be answered with a simple "yes" or "no." They value people's individual thoughts and ideas. They typically begin with "what" or "how." You can adjust the vocabulary, of course, to the age of the child or person you are talking to.

These help home in on the person's strengths and help create self-validation while always focusing forward:

- How did you learn to do that?
- Will you teach me how to do that?
- What are you feeling right now?
- What are you learning from those feelings?
- What did you learn from answering that question?
- What two or three things about that person/event/situation are you most pleased with?
- What areas of your performance are you most pleased with?
- In what ways are you looking forward to enhancing your performance during the next month/year?
- What do you feel are your greatest attributes?
- What have you done today that you would like to acknowledge yourself for?
- What do you think we should do?
- In what ways could I be most helpful to you right now?

The following are additional questions I think give valuable gifts to our children, including such qualities as creativity, analytical and critical thinking, problem solving, decision making, learning to acknowledge and accept other people's feelings, and possibly most important, simply thinking. That is, young people learn that every action has a consequence, whether good or bad, and given the choice, can head for the desired consequences as often as possible.

- How do you think you'll feel if you do that?
- What will likely happen if you do that? Are those the results you want most?
- How do you think so-and-so will feel if you do that?
- What are the qualities that cartoon (TV, movie, etc.) character has that you like the best?
- Who else will benefit if you do that?
- What other ways could we solve this problem?
- What do you think would happen if we did it this way?
- What would you do if:

—The door was locked one day and you couldn't get in the house;
—Someone offered you a ride home from school;
—I got lost and you couldn't find me in the mall;
—You made a special card for your grandma;
—You mowed the neighbor's lawn as a surprise;
—Your friend says it won't hurt to take this pill someone gave him;
—Your buddy wants to steal something from the store?

- How do you think other kids feel when someone does something like that to them?
- What do you think is the best way to handle this?
- What would be the value/consequences of that option?
- What will the ideal look like when it's complete?
- What part of that decision are you most comfortable about? Most uncomfortable about?
- What do we/you need to do to get where we/you would like to be?
- What are our resources for doing that?
- What are you most looking forward to in completing this task/project?
- What is the value to you when you complete this project?

- What would your favorite character be like if you made up a comic book (or book or TV show or movie)?
- Who would you invite to visit our house if you could choose anyone you want?
- AND WHAT DO YOU THINK WILL HAPPEN THEN? (This can be asked as a follow-up to any string of questions for as far out into time as the child can conceive at his age.)

"The teacher, if indeed wise,
does not bid you to enter
the house of their wisdom,
but leads you to the threshold
of your own mind."

—Kahlil Gibran

"Tell me and I'll forget;
Show me and I may remember;
Involve me and I'll understand."

—Chinese proverb

CHAPTER FOUR

Tool Four: Listen

The Listen Tool, like all the others, can be a make-or-break tool in our children's development. Here's a situation that had lifelong implications for a woman named Deanna.

> As a teenager I got absolutely no attention from my widowed mother. I had been programmed to believe that I shouldn't have been there, that I was a mistake. My mother's life basically ended when my father died, and she felt she had no reason to live. I was a nonentity to her.
>
> I was failing my senior year and had no self-worth. But at some point I decided to make an attempt to get through. I wanted to make my mother proud of me, to prove I was OK. I was failing social studies but I decided she might approve of me if I could pass it. I became totally absorbed in studying for a big test that was coming up.

The night before the final I asked Mom to quiz me on the material. The more things I answered right the better I felt. I began eagerly telling her everything I had learned. Suddenly I looked up, expecting her undivided attention and an acknowledgment of how proud she was of me.

She was asleep! I didn't even take my final the next day. Instead, I dropped out of high school.

That moment was my turning point. I could have gone one way or another. All I needed was for her to listen.

We could put up ten-foot banners around the house reminding our children how much we love them or how special they are, and yet these will have far less impact than a simple act of truly listening.

Cathy and Megan were best friends. They played together every day until last summer, when Megan died in a tragic accident in her family's swimming pool.

About a week after the accident, Megan's mother Joanne called Cathy's mom to thank her for her daughter's precious gift. It had been the most meaningful thing to happen to her since Megan's death.

Cathy's mother was confused. She didn't know Cathy had bought anything for Joanne. "What was it?" she asked.

Joanne replied, "Cathy came over to visit this morning to see how I was feeling. I tried to be brave and tell her that things were fine and that we were going to get over this eventually. But Cathy was wiser than that.

"She asked if she could sit in my lap like Megan used to do. Her gift was the next hour that she sat there and just listened to my pain and my memories. No one else has done that for me. We cried together, and hugged, and cried some

more—and Cathy just kept listening. Please thank her again for me."

It seems to me that listening ought to be one of the easiest things we do. It doesn't take any special equipment, we can do it standing up, sitting down, or completely prone. We don't have to think about making a point in a coherent, logical, grammatical manner as we might if we were speaking. All we have to do is listen.

But watching people "listen" often reminds me of "Telephone," one of my third-grade teacher's favorite rainy-day recess games. You may have played it too. The first person whispers a statement such as "My shirt is red" to the second person who repeats it in the ear of the next person, and so on down the line until everyone in the room has heard it whispered in their ear. The last person shouts out what he or she heard—which never failed to double us over with laughter because it usually came out something like "Uncle Charlie farts in the wind."

And we were really trying to listen!

Ever counted the number of times you replied "Yes, dear," or "Uh hunh," or "That was nice" to someone and a moment later couldn't remember what was said to you?

Ever noticed how many times you said those words while perusing the newspaper, watching TV, typing at the computer, peeling the potatoes or, worse yet, walking away from the person talking to you?

Research shows that you have a greater impact on people by how you listen than by what you say.

I used to be a master at that reading-the-newspaper-while-pretending-to-listen ploy. And then I had the audacity to wonder why my girls kept bugging me, getting louder and more physical in their attempts to get me to actually hear what they

"We could put up ten-foot banners around the
house reminding our children how much
we love them or how special they are,
and yet these will have far less impact
than a simple act of truly listening."

"Research shows that you have a greater impact
on people by how you listen
than by what you say."

"What kind of a message was I leaving
with my girls when I always
had a better idea?"

had to say. Suzie related a similar story when we talked about
the Listen Tool at a recent seminar:

> *I thought I was a great mom because we have a bedtime
> ritual of "Ten Minutes." That is, I spend ten minutes of
> special private time lying in bed with each child at bedtime.
> But I just realized I'm usually thinking about what time it
> is or what I'm going to do next and I have no idea what
> my child is saying. Starting tonight, I'm going to actually
> listen.*

Even if you maintain steady eye contact with someone,
you're still not really listening until you actually hear what
they're saying. That means listening until the person is finished,
paying attention to nonverbal clues, and not planning your response until the other person is finished talking.

In other words, catch the feeling. Understanding how the
child is feeling is often much more important to him than the
details he's relating.

My conversations with my children used to go a lot like this:

"Daddy, can we go to the park?"

"No."

"Daddy, Emmy's hitting me."

"Emmy, stop it."

"Daddy, Ali's got my toy."

"Ali, give it back."

"Daddy, can we . . ."

"Not now, sweetie, I'm busy."

My longer responses were filled with advice, mini-lectures,
moralizing, and hairy emotionalism. What kind of a message
was I leaving with my girls when I always had a better idea?
Long or short, each and every one of my reactions discounted
my daughters, cut them off from expressing their own feelings
and opinions, and guaranteed they'd never say anything of

value to me again because, clearly, I didn't care what they thought anyhow.

I can hardly believe we're the same family these days. Actually, we aren't the same family. Because we truly listen to each other now, we really know one another's thoughts and feelings. Before, we were just three people who passed data back and forth and maybe once in a while had some impact on each other.

For example, that question, "Daddy, can we go to the park?" now involves a discussion of when and where and with whom and for what purpose before we decide to go or not. Maybe she just needs to do something different for a while and it doesn't have to be a trip to the park. If I don't have the time to go all the way to the park, maybe spending five or ten minutes doing something around the house together might satisfy her real need.

When I remember to choose the high road, the statement, "Daddy, Emmy's hitting me" now gets a response such as: "You sound pretty mad. What are you mad about?" I listen and I acknowledge whatever they're feeling. I give love messages, I let them know I can see why they're upset. I conclude with comments such as: "I trust you to work out a good solution to the problem you're having. Let me know what you decide to do or how you work it out." No more rushing to rescue the younger one, no moralizing about how older sisters need to love and protect the younger kids, no imposition of adult solutions to the kids' problems.

I have a friend who's a public radio and books-on-tape addict. But you'll never find her with a radio on while she's doing something else. She reminds me of those old photos from the '30s and '40s where families are sitting around their radio and staring at it as we do these days with TV. She's also one of the best listeners I've ever met. As she says, if it's worth listening to, it's worth *listening* to. I agree, and add, who's more important to listen to than our family members?

When and how we listen can make such a difference. One delightful mom had a way to make sure her daughter knew what she had to say was vital, even when there was apparently no time to listen. "Is what you need to say important," GeraLine would ask, "or is it very, very, very important?" "If I got the 'very, very' routine, I'd stop whatever I was doing on the spot. Otherwise we set up another time when I could listen just as intently but not be distracted by the dinner boiling over."

Remember Hank and Nancy, the parents of little "Miss Adorable" I mentioned earlier? They had a 13-year-old who was giving them endless grief. She'd been a pleasant, well-behaved child until about 11, they said, and then everything went down the tubes. After attending a "10 Greatest Gifts" seminar they realized they hadn't actually listened to anything she had to say for at least two years.

For several weeks this family lasered in on listening to *everything* she had to say. This was not an easy process because, needless to say, once we stop listening, our kids stop talking. Or at least they stop saying anything much beyond "Pass the dessert" or "Where are the car keys?" If you think it's difficult to find the time to listen now, I assure you that the pain of being cut off from the essence of those beautiful children when they stop talking to you will make you wish you'd found the time or the willingness to listen earlier.

Hank and Nancy were absolutely committed to rediscovering the wonderful young woman they'd once known. They started with forward focus questions. They listened to her answers. They started to share their own feelings, which they had never shared with her before. They listened to her feelings—and most important, acknowledged each and every one as important to her, even when it was hard to understand why she could be upset about hair spray.

Instead of hurling orders at her as they had been, they listened to her reasoning as to how things might be done. Instead of slapping punishments on her, they listened to her idea of what appropriate consequences might be. Instead of thinking for her, instead of always imposing their "better idea" on her, they listened to her solutions to problems.

It didn't happen overnight, but within a month their daughter was a person they truly liked again. They discovered someone with hopes and fears and ideas they never would have known about, but that they delighted in once they found out. Plus they noticed her increased self-esteem, sense of responsibility, dignity, self-respect—and she, too, focused forward much more often.

Remember Deanna, whose story begins this chapter? When she became a parent, she found herself unconsciously repeating the same patterns she'd grown up with.

> There was a point in my life a few years ago when I was a single parent and was really busy trying to build my consulting business. I was very focused on helping people and trying to make enough money to support us. I had been called to be a panelist on a TV show and that added even more work to my load.
>
> One weekend while I was out helping people, one of my teenage daughters was raped. I never even knew there was a problem until a week and a half later when the principal brought her home and told me.
>
> It was a painful, excruciating way to realize I had been too busy to even listen to my children, to find out what was going on in my own family.

Another dad told us how angry he was with his daughter, who was going to a counselor to help resolve some family problems. "She shares everything with her counselor and never tells me anything. How can we work out anything if she won't talk to me?" he asked. When he finally asked his daughter, she said,

"Dad, I talk to him because he just listens. You give me all these lectures, and advice and put-downs. I don't want to share with you. It's too painful."

What happens when we don't listen at home? If we're lucky, a caring teacher will take the time to listen and to fill in some of the emptiness our children feel. If we're not, rest assured our kids will find someone to listen, maybe a gang member or a drug dealer or a smooth-talking partner who wants sex or, as the letter at the end of this chapter from a 15-year-old runaway says so eloquently—anyone who will listen.

Some kids in Houston were lucky. I caught a portion of a newscast recently where a former student was marveling that an athletic program that started with about 80 kids at the beginning of the school year had dwindled to 20, and then had suddenly swelled from 20 students back to 80. When he asked the new coach what wonderful innovations he had brought to the program, the coach stated simply: "I think they just needed somebody to care, to listen, to be there for them."

The gifts we give our children when we take the "high road" and really listen are incredible:

- We validate their feelings. How real can children feel if it seems that we never hear them? What message are they getting when responses to their statements go like this? "I'm not hungry." "Eat your dinner, now!" "I'm not sleepy." "Get into that bed and go to sleep." "I don't like my brother." "You've got to like him, he's your brother." It's the major complaint of people from dysfunctional families—they were never allowed to have real feelings. They grew up distrusting their own sense of the world and themselves. Their feelings and ideas were never okay.
- We enhance their self-esteem. When we truly listen we're acknowledging that they have something important to say and that we value their opinion.

- We encourage their problem-solving skills as we hear out their solutions.
- We foster their creativity as we let them recreate a scene or embellish it with detail.

The poignant letter on the next page was written by a 15-year-old runaway who expresses the pain of never having been listened to.

Dear Folks:

Thank you for everything—but I'm going to Chicago to try and start a new life. You asked me why I did those things and why I caused you so much trouble. The answer is easy for me to give you. But I am wondering if you will understand. Do you remember when I was about 6 or 7 and I used to want you to just listen to me? I remember all the nice things you gave me for Christmas and my birthday. And I was really happy with the things, for about a week.

But the rest of the time, I really didn't want presents, I just wanted you to listen to me like I was somebody who felt things too, because I remember even when I was young, I felt things. But you said you were busy. Dad, you had your career, and Mom, you're a wonderful cook and you had everything so clean. But you were both so tired so much from doing all of those things that made you busy—and you know something, Mom, I would have liked crackers and peanut butter just as well—if you had only sat down with me during the day for a while and said, "Tell me about it so maybe I can help you understand."

If my sister ever has children, I hope you will tell her to pay attention to the one who doesn't smile very much, because that one will really be crying inside. And, when she's about to bake six dozen cookies, to make sure first that the kids don't want to tell her about a dream . . . or a hope . . . or an idea . . . or a hurt . . . or something. Because thoughts are important to small kids too—even though they don't have so many words to use when they tell about what they have inside them.

I think that most of the things that kids are doing that parents are pulling out their hair worrying about . . . I think they're mostly just looking for someone who will have time to listen a few minutes and who really truly treats them with the same respect and attention they'd give a grown-up. If anybody asks you where I am, tell them I went looking for somebody with time because I have a lot of things I want to talk about.

CHAPTER FIVE

Tool Five: Model

A couple I know discovered firsthand how strong parental role models are as they stood paralyzed in a grocery checkout line one day in 1963. They'd dated each other all through their college years and thought they knew each other as well as any two people could. They got married the day before graduation, traveled for a few weeks and found an apartment.

The first day in their new place they went to the grocery store to stock up on food and supplies. It was the first time they'd ever shopped together. This is how Alice describes it:

> It might have been the last time we ever shopped together too—if we hadn't figured out how ridiculous the whole situation was.
>
> Choosing things was a breeze. I knew he liked chocolate but not caramel sauce on ice cream; he didn't care what color ironing board cover I wanted. We arrived at the check-

out stand with our laden cart and calmly watched the clerk ring up our purchases. We then proceeded to make all the people in line behind us wish they'd chosen any other lane in the store.

The clerk announced the total and waited for payment. She waited some more. More time passed. I was blissfully unaware as I stood double-checking my list, staring at nothing in particular, and waiting for the order to be bagged. My husband was doing pretty much the same. It took a long while before we realized no one was paying for our stuff.

I looked at my husband and wondered why he wasn't writing out a check. We had plenty of money. He looked at me and wondered the same thing. We looked at each other some more. The clerk's irritation was getting pretty obvious.

I forget who finally broke the impasse and actually paid for the order. But one thing became immediately clear. There we were—the spitting image of our parents. You see, my husband's father brought home his paycheck each week, handed it over to his wife, and she handled all the family finances. The exact reverse was true in my family. My father paid for everything. My husband never knew the man could pay for the groceries, I never knew the woman could.

Our children absorb behaviors and attitudes and language every waking minute of their lives. And even though they may spend time in day-care or with baby-sitters, you, the parent, are still the most important person in their lives. The number-one way children learn is to mimic, and who better to mimic than their most important person?

I first realized how much our kids pattern themselves after us when we got a new puppy a few years ago. I looked up from doing the dishes and saw my girls on the floor playing with the puppy. It was like watching a three- and five-year-old hologram of me. They petted the puppy like I did, they played with it like I did, they spoke to it like I did. I could predict their every action. Once I started looking, I noticed that they cleaned up their rooms the same way I did, they talked to their friends just as I talked to mine.

I had great fun recently watching a momma cat herding her new kittens around. I soon realized that she is not just a food bar for the little ones. Everything she does is aimed at teaching her offspring how to become a perfect adult of the species. Kittens are born with some instinctual behaviors, but it's up to momma to teach them litterbox manners and how to groom themselves, how to protect themselves from danger.

While momma cat is teaching the somewhat limited range of behaviors her kittens need to know for survival, we human parents are doing the same thing with our children. While potty training, good grooming, and protection from danger are as important for humans as they are for our pets, we want our children to know much more than survival techniques.

And they will learn much, much more, whether or not you know you're consciously teaching it. I'm sure you frequently wonder where on earth they picked up this habit or that mannerism. At least you'll wonder until you realize that the most perfect mirrors in the world are not finely silvered pieces of glass—they are our children. When you look at them, you are looking at yourself. As one astute observer noted: "Out of the mouths of babes come the words we never should have said in the first place."

A parent in one of our "10 Greatest Gifts" seminars first realized how important her actions were in shaping her child's behaviors after a very simple act. As they left the bathroom one day, she stooped to straighten the bathroom rug which had gotten crumpled against the tub. Every time the rug was out of

"The most perfect mirrors in the world are not
finely silvered pieces of glass
—they are our children.
When you look at them, you are looking
at yourself."

"Modeling is one of the most important,
yet simple, parenting tools you can use.
It's a tool that keeps working even when
you're not around because your children
see how your life is working, what kind of results
you create by the way you live.
Remember, your children cannot hear what you
say until they see what you do."

"Just as no one can ever really define love,
children still know exactly what it means by how
they see you live love—or any of the other gifts
you want them to have."

place after that, her two-year-old stooped to straighten it—and place it exactly where she had. Goodness, she thought, if he picked that up in one quick moment, think what he'd gotten over the past two years watching the things she did over and over again.

Do you think your family has some secrets? Surprise! You haven't hung around your child's preschool enough or listened to your kids play "house" or "school" or "office" or wherever their imagination takes them.

Ask any teacher. They know exactly how you talk on the telephone, how you talk to each other, what and how you eat, what your politics are, how you handle conflict, how you treat your pets, your favorite gestures—and all they've done is observe your children. Your attitudes are an open book.

At one of Bill Clinton's inaugural events, Barbra Streisand asked what the message was to the children in "Hansel and Gretel" when they were sent out in the woods to die. Her following question struck a responsive chord in me. She asked, "What message are you giving your children—and others—by sending them out in the world with your attitudes?"

> One mom discovered that her 13-year-old son was lying about his age so he could still get into movies for the children's price. She made sure he heard plenty about honesty from both her and his dad.
>
> The next week her son accompanied her to the transmission shop where her car had been towed when it broke down the day before. The mechanic presented them with the bad news: It would take at least $2000 to fix the car. But the good news was that it was all work that would be covered under the warranty.
>
> The really bad news they discovered when they checked the warranty was that it had expired the week before.
>
> "Don't worry," the mechanic said. "I can fudge the date

on the work order by a few days so it would come under
warranty." The mother agreed immediately.

As they were leaving the shop, her son turned and
asked, "So, Mom, is there a two-thousand-dollar limit on
honesty?"

When we were talking about the tool of modeling at a seminar, one couple related that their kids' favorite game is "Hi, honey, I'm home." They and the whole group suddenly realized how much they were modeling for their children: how to have a relationship, create a household, how to talk, how to listen, how to resolve conflict, how to raise kids, how to treat a friend—or someone who's not a friend. In essence, their blueprint for how to be a human on the planet earth comes from you, the parents.

I'll bet I even know precisely when you first realized how much you've modeled your own parents, even though you've deliberately done everything differently, even though you've vowed you'd never, ever be like THEM. I'll bet that moment came when, despite all your protestations to the contrary, you first opened your mouth as a parent and found your parents' exact words floating out. It's that cosmic two-by-four slap to your head when you utter: "Oh no, I sound just like my mother."

It's not necessarily bad to sound like your mother. Most of our mothers—and fathers—were trying their hardest to create perfect little citizens who would grow up to be happy, fulfilled, independent adults. What's bad is if they sounded just like their parents, who unconsciously did just what their parents did, and so on for generations—and you are repeating patterns you'd like to change without knowing how to choose new ways.

Maybe you've heard this old story about the Easter ham.

Every year a family carefully chose a large ham for their
holiday dinner, but the mother always cut off the end before

she baked it. One year the daughter hosted the meal and her new husband asked why she cut off the end of the ham before she cooked it. "Because that's the way my mother always did it," she said.

"I don't know why either," her mother replied when they asked her. "But that's the way my mother always did it."

Everybody at this point was curious enough to call the grandmother to ask her why she cut the end of the ham off before cooking it.

"Simple," she responded. "I never had a baking pan big enough to hold the whole ham."

How much of our parenting style still cuts the end off our children's "ham"?

How many times do we still do things the "same old way" even when that way may not be the best way any more?

I have noticed in my own life that I frequently have a hard time consistently using these tools the new way. I have a tendency to jump right in and say "No" or "Don't" or to find what's wrong or give orders.

On a recent trip to Disneyland, I found some of the foreign visitors really irritating in their push to be first in line, their loud talk and other (at least to my mind) rude behaviors. I also found that the more I focused on their obnoxiousness, the fewer good traits I could see. This was really ruining my fun with my girls, I thought, and decided to get a grip on the only thing I could control—my own focus.

The girls and I started to talk to every foreign visitor we could, asking them where they were from, about their vacation, what they liked best about their homeland. Soon the girls were front and center asking questions and sharing the excitement of knowing new people. Instead of passing on my old stereotyped attitudes, my kids were learning the

priceless gifts of finding the good in people, learning equal-
ity, acceptance, and more.

When I was back in Nebraska recently, I got a clear picture
of where that tendency to react in the old way came from.

After a few days at my parents' house, my daughter Ali
asked a very pointed question. "Daddy," she asked, "how come
everything Grandma does makes you feel good but Grandpa
says things that make you feel bad?"

She'd noticed the put-downs, the negative comments, the
judgments that were his pattern for years and years. All my life,
it seems, I was never noticed for doing things right. I know he
had the best of all loving intentions, but the minute I stepped off
the path and did something wrong or not up to snuff—wham! I
heard about it.

I know where he got that parenting style. He was modeling
his own mother, who I remember always using the same back-
side-of-the-energy-circle approach to life. It was a transgenerational style that passed right on through to me.

I approached my dad during this vacation because I was
feeling the painful effects of those old habits both physically
and mentally. I said to him, "Papa, I know you would do anything in the world for me, but since I've been here you've only
noticed the things I've done wrong or that weren't up to your
standards. You've criticized my ideas, my kids, and me. It's really starting to hurt."

He shifted considerably after that conversation. And I admire him even more because it takes a strong person to make
that kind of change.

A friend of mine went through a lot of soul searching and
expensive therapy in her early 30s, following her divorce.

I'd flat run out of "script" for my life as a divorced
woman. All the women in my family married, had children,

stayed home to raise them, outlived their husbands, and then eventually moved in with their children for the last years of their lives.

I'd already broken the mold by having a career, and then going back to work a few months after we adopted a baby. Now I was on my own and I had no role models whatsoever, and not enough self-esteem to think that I could invent who-ever I wanted to be or, better yet, just be who I was. Who was I? Without those convenient and comfortable well-defined roles of wife and mother, I had absolutely no clue.

I started rereading all the novels I'd read in the '50s which had helped shape my idea of being a woman different from those in my family. I found the same tired stereotypes cropping up. Primarily, you were a Good Woman, i.e., young, beautiful, and married with perfect children. Some women were allowed to have careers, but always in menial jobs, and they always found the Perfect Man before the last chapter.

More likely the working woman was a poor suffering widow who was forced to work to support herself and her perfect children. Or you were a Bad Woman, middle-aged, divorced and drunk most of the time. Old women weren't even mentioned unless they were wealthy and/or amus-ingly eccentric. That era's movies touted the same basic party line.

I don't wish for a minute that someone in my family be-fore me had gotten divorced so I could see how it was done. But it was painful—and expensive—as an adult to fill in the gaps of qualities and strengths that were missing from my childhood, qualities that would have allowed me to think through a new life for myself when there were no role models to follow.

I don't blame my parents at all. They were wonderful

people who did their best raising us. We always had an abundance of good food, stylish clothes, and exciting vacation travel. We went to Scout camp, Sunday School, and all got college educations. Big family get-togethers were frequent.

Along with all this wonderful stuff, I also got lots of telling: when I was supposed to study, what to wear and where to go and with whom. I remember a continuous message was: "You did OK on this grade card but couldn't you get A+ instead of just an A?" I never seemed to measure up, so who I was obviously wasn't good enough.

What I also didn't get was a sense that I could think for myself, that I could take care of myself, that I could solve problems, that I could be different from other people, that it was OK to be a unique individual. No one ever asked me, "How would you do this?" or "What do you think about that?" It seemed only the adults were allowed to know the answers.

I was a bright student and always knew the answer when quizzed about a fact from the textbook or the solution to the problem on the board. I could do brilliant book reviews as long as no one wanted to know what I actually thought about the book. I didn't know I could think. I remember wondering how people could have opinions. I thought critics were the smartest people in the world because they actually had opinions about things.

The best metaphor for my life was how I shut myself off from ever taking art classes after I nearly flunked seventh-grade art. The teacher had the gall to ask us to use our imagination. I didn't know I had one, so I made sure I never got back into anything as frustrating as that again. Everybody had always told me to stay in the lines when I colored and I was a good little girl.

As a parent you are constantly modeling life to your children, shaping a majority of their behaviors, attitudes, mannerisms, speech patterns, problem-solving techniques—the list is endless. Experts say our children get 90 percent of their behavior and values from us.

You are the one who creates their operations manual for life. The important point is whether you are using the tool of modeling the "old" way as an unconscious zombie, or the "new" way by being consciously aware of what you are doing.

It's great fun to see our infant children mimic our smiles; it's not so entertaining when our toddlers yell out our favorite profanity in front of Grandma or at Sunday School. It's delightful to hear them answer the telephone in a soft gracious tone like we do; it's agonizing to hear them scream at a pet or a playmate the same way we do when we're out of control.

Many of us were surprised recently when a 16-year-old friend of a neighborhood girl was fatally shot while trying to rob a liquor store. We knew he'd had some problems in his life and that he'd run up some debts, but we had hoped he would work it out. A couple of days later we learned his father had just fled the country to avoid some problems with the IRS. We were not so surprised when we realized what kind of modeling—or lack of it—he had in problem-solving.

I watched one day as a divorced dad was talking to his son on the phone. He heard his former wife yell in the background that they had to go now. She grabbed the phone away from the little boy, told my friend they had to go and slammed the receiver down. The clear message was that neither the child nor his dad was important, that the mother's schedule took precedence. I can well imagine this young man growing up to treat his mom or his friends with the same lack of respect as the pattern she's modeled.

I'm reminded of the story about the farmer who got first prize at the county fair for growing a pumpkin the exact size and shape of a two-gallon jug. When asked how he'd done that he said, "I put the pumpkin blossom in the jug and let it grow that way."

Aren't our lives the same? The vision we have of ourselves is how we'll grow. Parents are crucial in creating the "jug" or mold for their children's lives.

One couple at a seminar wondered what their neighbors' child would be like in a few years since his parents always refer to him as "Our little attack baby." I love the bumper stickers that proclaim "Our child is an honor student at such-and-such middle school." I want to scream when I see the stickers that say "My child just beat up your honor student." Is it any wonder we see so much childhood violence if this is the model these parents have created for their children?

So many principals have told me how they shudder as parents bring their children in for the first day of kindergarten, or when transferring them into the school and announce: "You'll have trouble with this one. He's a little brat." Or, "You let me know the first minute little Miss Sassy opens her mouth."

These parents can rest assured their children will probably do exactly what they expect.

But, you say, once they go to school, or watch TV or go to the movies, they pick up all that disgusting stuff from their peers. What we do at home isn't all that important anymore.

Of course, you'll still have to put up with "Cowabunga" reverberating through your house, gyrating little pelvises aping the latest MTV or post-touchdown moves, experimental language spewing out of their little mouths, and weird haircuts. Children need to experiment with different styles of dress and behavior as they explore who they are and what they really want and need.

As you saw in previous chapters, your messages and your willingness to ask questions and truly listen to their answers will make a vast difference in whether the experimentation runs a harmless course or the kids feel they have to carry it to further and further extremes to resist you. In the absence of positive modeling and response at home, our children *will* find their role models at school, on TV or on the streets.

You can consciously choose the way you live your life, the way you consistently present your truth, the way you serve as a model to your children as an ideal adult of the species. Modeling is one of the most important, yet simple, parenting tools you can use. It's a tool that keeps working even when you're not around because your children see how your life is working, what kind of results you create by the way you live.

Remember, your children cannot hear what you say until they see what you do.

There is no end to the list of qualities and values you give your children by modeling. A minister once told me, "We are the only gospel our neighbors need to read." I realized fully then that the way we live our lives is the gospel our children study. What is the message if we tell them not to lie and then they hear us on the phone giving a phony reason why we don't want to do something? Or we tell them to obey the rules and they watch us drive over the speed limit?

Conversely, just as no one can ever really define love, children still know exactly what it means by how they see you live love—or any of the other gifts you want them to have.

As one mom at a seminar said so beautifully: "I am going to model the kind of parent I want to be."

When we first see our children, we all have dreams about the kind of family we want to raise. We want them to grow up happier and even more successful than we. We want them to have high self-esteem, integrity, to care about others and to make a difference on the planet.

And then we meet life head on. We so easily can get overwhelmed with schedules, finances, chores, to-do lists, and careers. I believe that the number-one way to give your dream is to live it—be the kind of person you want your children to become.

Participants in our "10 Greatest Gifts" seminars go through a special process to create a unique family vision and to define the gifts they want to nurture in their children to support that vision.* That work is crucial and very special, because the power of your vision can transform you and your family beyond your greatest expectations! Remember, we go toward what we focus on.

I went through so many years as a parent never realizing that I could create a vision for my family; never realizing I could give the gifts of qualities and values that fit that vision to my children as easily as I could take care of their physical needs. The icing on the cake was to wake up from my zombie state and realize how important my own life was in getting the message across to them. To paraphrase a common saying, "What you live is what you get."

---

* For more information regarding the "10 Greatest Gifts" project, including research, articles, newsletters, joyshops, seminars, and keynote addresses, please call 800-569-1877 or write to: The 10 Greatest Gifts Project, P.O. Box 5301, Denver, CO 80217, or see page 272 for further information.

"More than $1.4 billion per year of new juvenile de-
tention facilities and prisons are not stanching the
growing alienation among our young, who lack a
purposeful, joyful song to sing in life—
a song that is learned first in the home
and reinforced in school and in
other community institutions and by
the religious and political values and climates in
our society. Too many of our children are adrift
today because too many parents, other adults
and political and business leaders give no
thought to teaching by positive example.
James Baldwin was right when he said
our children do not follow words,
but our actions."

(From *The Measure of Our Success* by Marian Wright
Edelman, 1992. Reprinted by permission of Beacon Press.)

CHAPTER SIX

Parenting from the Heart

What do you think all five of these parenting tools—focus, listen, teach, messages, model—have in common? When we asked that question at one of our first seminars, one mother's hand shot up and she shouted: "This is parenting from the heart." She had barely finished when another parent said, "Maybe this is what love really is. If we don't treat our families this way, are we really demonstrating love?"

Have you started to see how using each of these tools in the "new" way could enhance your family, your classroom, or any other interactions you have with children? How you still can handle all the day-to-day issues that come up while keeping a clear vision of what the child is receiving from the interaction? How you can consciously choose the gifts that your child will receive from everything you do and say to each other?

How would your family or classroom or neighborhood be different if you did the following every day:

- Focus forward on what is going well, on your family's accomplishments and pleasures and anticipation of good things to come, on knowing you can solve the problems that do come up.
- Listen with full attention to your child's thoughts and feelings and stories.
- Teach through discovery, letting each child learn his own best path.
- Give enhancing and empowering messages. Catch your kids being good and acknowledge and celebrate even the smallest behavior that's part of your overall vision for them.
- Model your own sense of worth, your own power to consciously choose what you will focus on, how much you have to share with your family and the world.

Remember the mother we talked about earlier whose hassles with her three-year-old each morning were driving her crazy? Here's how she put all five tools together to solve her ongoing problem.

> Becky decided to use each tool to get their morning off to a good start and leave her daughter with some lifetime gifts in the process. First she used the Teach Tool and asked questions rather than telling Melissa what she wanted done. (Remember, it's almost impossible for kids to fight against decisions they've made themselves. When was the last time you rebelled against one of your own good ideas?)
>
> The night before she would ask Melissa what she thought she would feel like tomorrow. Would she rather dress "frilly" or "practical"? Did she think she might like to wear a dress or her jeans? Jeans, OK. Which pair did she prefer? Step by step, they'd lay out her wardrobe for the next day.
>
> Step by step, Becky continued to listen to her daughter, to validate her feelings and choices. She shifted Melissa's focus

*to thinking and planning ahead, to anticipating a good day
because she'd made such good choices ahead of time. Becky
modeled appropriate behavior by laying out her own clothes
for the next day. Finally, she gave lots and lots of love messages, acknowledging Melissa for each behavior, no matter
how small, that made their mornings go smoothly.*

Becky was brimming with enthusiasm when she called to
tell us the problem was solved.

*You know, I knew the old way was not working, but I
had no idea the old way was actually killing her potential.
The new way is encouraging and enhancing it.*

*I can't believe I paid money to learn this. This is so sim-
ple. This is really about core issues, about treating our children with dignity and respect. This is really living the
Golden Rule, not just giving it lip service.*

*But you know, you're going to have a hard time getting
the word out on this because we've all been taught so differently. We're all so certain our job as parents is to tell our
kids everything, to point out their problems and what they
have to work on. Parents are going to have to discover the
cost of what they're doing and how they're destroying their
families with the old ways.*

Remember the fable of the farmer who found a goose that
laid golden eggs? After a few days, the farmer's greed overcame
him and he killed the goose so he could get all the eggs at once instead of having to wait for another one each day. Just as he killed
off his potential for more eggs, we parents can get just as short-
sighted when we focus only on taking care of our children's
physical needs. I remember that my parents, like everyone else's,
always warned me to wear clean underpants when I went out. I
would have also appreciated more concern that I enjoy the day or

"This is really living the Golden Rule,
not just giving it lip service."

"True spirituality can't be programmed to happen
between 9 and 11 A.M. during the church
service. Parenting can't be scheduled either—
it's totally unpredictable.
What this approach does guarantee
is that every interaction we have together will
not destroy my family but will nurture
appropriate qualities and values."

learn from it or whatever. But just like them, as a dad I was so concerned about keeping the kids fed, keeping them warm and all their other physical needs, I wasn't even aware of how much I could impact their emotional selves as well.

An increasing number of hospital staff agree that they've focused exclusively on feeding techniques, diapers, and babies' physical surroundings—all very important—but now need to give new parents much more information on emotional needs too.

Does knowing about and using these tools make you a perfect parent? Sorry, I haven't figured that out yet for myself, much less how to pass sainthood on to anyone else. It's so easy to drift back into old, unconscious habits. As soon as I find myself doing that, I stop, FAC myself for noticing I was doing it and continue using one or more of the tools the new way.

One of our seminar leaders found herself in that same situation just the other day. Over the years she and her son have enjoyed visiting all sorts of factories and studios and workplaces —"anywhere that will tour us through their facilities so we can see what makes the world work behind the scenes," she says.

This time, while her son was home from college for the holidays, they decided to see how the postal system moves the mail. It was a state-of-the-art facility with much computerized sorting and dispatching, but also still a lot of manual loading and unloading of trays, bins, and entire trucks.

As they finished an hour-and-half tour of the postal facility, she asked him what he thought of it. Her son, who loves physical activity, admitted that he might like to work there for a while. She immediately lost whatever vestiges of new parenting style she had, and launched into a lecture about how this was the very reason people went to college, to avoid dead-end grunt labor jobs, how boring the work there was.

"We're all so certain our job as parents
is to tell our kids everything,
to point out their problems
and what they have to work on.
Parents are going to have to discover
the cost of what they're doing
and how they're destroying their families
with the old ways."

"The new century doesn't begin for a few years, but
what we do this week, this day,
this minute will create the way
that new century looks."

It took her a couple of hours to realize she'd been a perfect model of an old, low-road parent. She'd completely stopped listening when he said something she didn't like. She didn't acknowledge his feelings and desires. She denied his truth. Everything she said about boring and dead-end jobs was true for her but might not bear any resemblance at all to what he or thousands of workers like to do.

She approached him with an apology and asked if they could rerun the conversation because she really was interested in what he thought. They did, and her son's happy grin as she left the room was the best gift he could ever give her.

To me, these five tools are the guarantee that I'll truly parent from the heart. I can't always remember which parenting technique to use in which situation. I know my kids don't learn trust or creativity or integrity through a lecture or a planned family activity.

As a good friend of mine often says, true spirituality can't be programmed to occur between 9 and 11 A.M. during the church service. Parenting can't be scheduled either—it's totally unpredictable. I have no idea what the next situation's going to be— an incident at school, a broken window, an accident or health problem. What this approach does guarantee is that every interaction we have together will not destroy my family but will nurture appropriate qualities and values.

Does it always work? No, but does anything else always work? Not that I've found.

Even when this approach doesn't work as immediately as I'd like it to, at least I know that I'm not bankrupting my children's future, that I am giving them the qualities and values they need long-term.

Leaders everywhere today are focusing on the hope and promise of the next millennium. Despite our attention on the environment, our standard of living, health care, our corporations or the direction of our government, I firmly believe there is an important element missing if we don't cultivate a new vision for our children and our families.

The new century doesn't begin for a few years, but what we do this week, this day, this minute will create the way that new century looks. Our efforts will require the wisdom and lessons of our adults as well as the dreams and promise and magic of children.

A lot of our old parenting methods—focusing on the "spots," using "No" and "Don't" frequently, telling instead of questioning, listening only so we can jump in with our own better ideas—destroy the power and potential of this much needed intergenerational process. Let's allow our children to flourish as we grow together to the new millennium!

For the rest of this book, I'd like to share 10 of the greatest gifts I can ever give my children. There are many, many more, but these are among the ones I am willing to go to the ends of the earth to see that my daughters receive.

"What lies behind us and what lies before us
are tiny matters
compared to what lies within us."

—Oliver Wendell Holmes

"When I'm mad, my heart feels pounding
like I'm stuffing it up.
When I'm glad, I feel all lit up.
My heart feels like it's getting
whatever it wants."

—Alison Vannoy, age 7

"When I'm mad, I feel like I want to scream,
but I know that won't do any good.
I just want to put everyone down,
I want to take it out on someone else,
but I know that won't do any good either.
I think of something happy,
something to look forward to
so I'll be happy.
When I'm glad I feel like I'm about to float up in the air,
like a butterfly is lifting me
from inside."

—Emily Vannoy, age 9

CHAPTER SEVEN

The Gift of Feeling Fully

Feeling fully, to me, means life itself. Knowing and experiencing their emotions is a gift I want with all my heart for my children.

Feelings are like a river. If we stuff them up, our emotional stream becomes stagnant, dirty, disease-ridden. It's like trying to build barriers against the mighty Mississippi. Eventually the flood builds and breaks through in wrenching, destructive ways, as it did so tragically in the summer of '93. When people break we get mayhem, even murder, and certainly expensive therapy bills. When we allow our feelings to flow freely, we're cleansing our system. Our minds are clear and our lives are a joy to live.

Feeling fully is essential to growing and learning, to health, to living. Otherwise we're on automatic pilot, operating out of old patterns and belief systems. We are not fully experiencing life.

Feeling fully means not being afraid of our feelings. Feelings crop up all day, every day. If you think of our lives as the sky, feelings are the clouds that float through it. They may obscure the bright light of the sun from time to time; they may even appear to fill up the sky for days on end. But they'll always float on past, and the degree to which we experience those feelings will help them move through even faster. If we ignore or block them, however, they will almost certainly gather negative energy and produce thunder and lightning, and rain or hail.

What happens when we carelessly put our finger too near a flame? The burning feeling in our finger is an unavoidable message to move it. We can't ignore that feeling or we'd burn our fingers off. I always knew enough to pay attention to physical feelings, but learning to do the same with emotional feelings has been a long process for me.

An incident with an elderly woman painfully reminded me of the need to honor our feelings.

> I'd parked outside the grocery store to run in for a couple of items. The girls wanted to stay in the car to continue listening to a tape and finish a game they were playing with their dolls.
>
> When I came back out to the car I was horrified to see my girls, their mouths hanging nearly to their knees in amazement, being bounced up and down in their seats from repeated impacts to the far side of the car. Someone was evidently trying to park in the space next to me. But instead of pulling smoothly into what seemed to be an ample parking space, this car swept in, bashed into mine, pulled back, adjusted a tad and swept back in again—leaving uniform dings every inch along the entire driver's side of my new car.
>
> I was livid. How could anyone that incompetent be allowed on the streets? Worse yet, how could anyone do this

kind of damage to another car and be so apparently oblivious to it? And still worse, how could anyone do that to two innocent little kids?

The object of my rage was a little old lady with poor vision. She took responsibility for the damage the minute it was pointed out to her and assured me her insurance company would take care of it. I immediately starting stuffing my anger.

I spent the rest of my day consumed by a massive headache. I was tired and grouchy. I yelled at the kids and kicked the dog. I had a stiff neck. I eventually realized that it wasn't the incident that made me so sick—it was my refusal to feel or express the emotions I had about it.

I explained this to the girls and they let me rant and rave, knowing that I was not angry with them. I honored my own emotional reaction without making myself a pathetic victim of the incident. Within a few minutes I—and the girls and the dog—felt so much better.

I remember going to a friend's farm when I was little. If he cried, instead of getting the comfort and attention he needed, people treated him like a wart. "Stop that or I'll give you something to cry about," was a phrase I often heard over there.

For the next few hours my friend was no longer fun to be with. He lost his joy and confidence as he retreated into shame and fear. He was no longer the friend I knew.

I remember what it did to me too. Our fun ended as I'd tiptoe around his father in fear of his wrath coming down on me.

When I was a child, I was always afraid of being found out, always running a little scared. I was convinced people wouldn't like me, that I wouldn't know the answer, I wasn't good enough, or that group of kids didn't want me in their crowd. Many times when I didn't know how to do something, I'd feel

"Feeling fully, to me, means life itself. Knowing
and experiencing their emotions is a gift I want
with all my heart for my children."

"Feelings are like a river. If we stuff them up,
our emotional stream becomes stagnant,
dirty, disease-ridden.
When we allow our feelings to flow freely,
we're cleansing our system.
Our minds are clear and our lives
are a joy to live."

tears welling up, but I'd snuff them quickly so the grown-ups wouldn't think I was stupid or weak. I had to act brave all the time.

I perpetuated the same pattern when my kids were young. I didn't know how to deal with my own feelings so, of course, I didn't know how to deal with theirs. I'd get furious when they were whining or crying. I'd order them to shape up, forcing them to stuff their pain or frustration and things would get ten times worse. Children will only escalate their behavior when we force them to deny who they really are or what they are really feeling.

When I thought my job was to be King Dad, I thought my ideas and feelings were dominant and everyone else was supposed to feel the same way. I was a fixer, a controller. Now I realize how much of their precious life I prevented my children from feeling and living fully.

Today, I frequently use a pregnant pause when I'm listening to them. It keeps me from saying something stupid like "How can you be hungry?" or "How can you be angry?" when they say they are. Of course they have every right to feel hungry or angry or whatever they feel. Feelings simply can't be argued about. How they act out their feelings is subject to firm guidelines; how they're feeling is simply not open to question.

A few minutes ago, Emmy and Ali came into my office as I was working on the phone. They felt bored and lonely. Before, I would have yelled that I was on the phone and for them to go away. The situation would only have escalated. Since we go toward what we focus on, they would have only gotten louder and more disruptive.

Today I encouraged them to come in. They just wanted to be close for a few minutes. I said, "I'm glad you're here, thanks for being quiet." Ali started a drawing and Emmy played dominoes on the floor. What a joyful difference—in my life and theirs!

We can only go forward if we honor where we are now. If we deny what we're really feeling, we're subconsciously telling ourselves that what we're feeling is wrong. And then we are firmly stuck on the back side of the energy circle because our automatic reaction is to defend our position. We can only go forward and live and love and enjoy life if we can acknowledge it's OK to be where we are now—otherwise we will only go backward, focusing on what's wrong or who did us wrong or what the problem is.

My friend Allison shared an incident that illustrated the need to honor feelings. Joseph and Gianna let their three-year-old Bridger work through his emotional upset while keeping a steady stream of love messages and priceless qualities and values coming his way.

> Bridger was furious that his mom wasn't going to let him have another Popsicle that hot summer afternoon. She quietly reminded him of their family guidelines for treats. He responded with typical toddler aggression. The struggle ended up with the refrigerator door hitting his mom on the head.

> I cringed in my seat waiting for what I so often see as a typical response to that kind of situation. Parent screams at the child for being bad, orders the kid out of the room and tells him not to come back until he's ready to act right. And on top of it, no more Popsicles for a month! Or worse yet, the parent lashes back at the child with a physical response such as a slap or a spanking. The child is left with the messages that he's bad, he's unlovable, and conflict is to be avoided or punished instead of resolved.

> Gianna is not that kind of parent. She expressed her anger and pain with a yell that was enough to get Bridger's attention. She used empowering love messages to express

how much that whack from the door hurt her head. She told
him she needed to feel angry for a few minutes because of
the situation. She told him he could stay around or go out-
side for a bit and then they would talk about it. She also ac-
knowledged that it was OK for him to feel angry that he
couldn't have everything he wanted, but that it was not OK
to get into a physical struggle over it.

Outside, his dad also honored the little guy's angry feel-
ings and again reminded him that it was OK to be angry
but it was not acceptable to hurt someone out of anger. He
also acknowledged that it was OK that Bridger felt hungry.
Joseph focused on the forward side of the energy circle by
asking what else there was around the house that would be
good to eat or drink.

The confrontation was over in just a couple of minutes as
the little boy went off to get a piece of fruit and a glass of water.
Since anger does so often stimulate the need for physical release, both mom and dad spent a few minutes playing ball with
the toddler to focus that energy into something positive and
fun. Bridger's self-esteem remained intact and he learned many
valuable lessons about feelings, conflict, family interaction, and
appropriate behavior.

My friend Don says that if we're stuck on expectations, we
can't enjoy the here and now. I believe if we expect that we're
supposed to feel a certain way, then we're not fully alive, we
can't enjoy the gifts and lessons, the "nowness," of where we
are and what we are doing.

Cindy and Bill told us about a pattern they changed with
their two-and-a-half-year-old daughter.

Our daughter used to get mad at her dad a lot. I would
always tell her, "Look, you got your dad upset. Go tell him

"Children will only escalate their behavior
when we force them to deny
who they really are
or what they are really feeling."

"Can you imagine a baby feeling guilty
about being angry or crying
from discomfort? Not at all.
Babies simply let their feelings out—
through screams, wails, giggles or wiggles—
and then focus on the next thing
in a blink of an eye.
What a lesson!"

you're sorry." Not only was I putting all the blame on her (which may or may not actually have been the case), I was also dictating what she should do to rectify the matter.

Now, we just let her feel mad and acknowledge that the feeling is OK. She calms down almost immediately and spontaneously goes over and hugs her dad.

Feelings are a gift. The only time they are harmful is if we deny them and feel guilty about them or we let them out in an unhealthy way. Feelings let us know ourselves. I'm finally starting to know who I am after years of shutting myself off from myself. Feelings are my biggest teacher; they let me know when it's time for change. If I stuff them or tell myself they're bad, I can't refocus and go forward.

Babies are masters at experiencing their feelings, expressing them—usually at top voice—and then letting them go. Can you imagine a baby feeling guilty about being angry or crying from discomfort? Not at all. Babies simply let their feelings out—through screams, wails, giggles or wiggles—and then focus on the next thing in a blink of an eye. What a lesson!

I am always amazed at the ability of a poet friend to express herself and her feelings. I asked how she became so expressive, when so many of us don't even know our feelings, let alone being able to share them.

My parents constantly honored my feelings, she explained. One of the most frequent things I heard was "Come over and sit on my lap and tell me what you're thinking and feeling." Even at age three I was consulted on how I felt about the family moving. My feelings always counted.

In contrast, I think of a young man in the film *Dead Poets Society*, the one who had to live up to the model created by his father. The boy killed himself when he wasn't allowed to have his own feelings, ideas or needs. Everyone focused on what was wrong with him. His dad was firmly stuck on the back side of the circle, always pointing out his son's mistakes, always seeing his spots.

Today, teenage suicide rates are rising dramatically. These tragedies didn't happen because these children are terminally ill or in financial desperation. In my opinion, they happen because our youth are emotionally impoverished.

A school principal told me that just ten years ago in 1984, she worried about gum in school—now it's guns. Every teacher I've consulted agrees that the need for gangs would go away if kids were only treated with respect and dignity and listened to at home—if we saw their beauty instead of their spots, if we began to accept them for who they are and what they feel.

Often in a dysfunctional family, kids aren't allowed to think what they think, feel what they feel, or say what they want to say. They constantly have to conform to someone else's ideas or moods. They are expected to walk the line for whoever's in charge.

What kind of a functional family would we create if we always used the five parenting tools? If we asked our family members, "What do you feel? What are your ideas? What do you think?" What if we listened without blocks or put-downs and honored their feelings as an expression of who they really are? If we modeled healthy, appropriate ways to express emotions? What if we always focused on their strengths instead of their shortcomings? I can think of no better formula for creating a fully functional family.

Honoring our children's feelings, however, doesn't mean we have to deny our own.

We went back to Nebraska recently for my 25th high-school reunion. The night came for the big party and Ali did not want me to go. My old, low-road parent would have yelled at her that she couldn't tell me what to do or screamed at her for being so selfish.

Instead, I told her how important this event was to me because it only happened once in a lifetime and that I was very excited to get a chance to see my old friends. And I listened deeply to how she felt. The minute I acknowledged her feelings —instead of forbidding them—they stopped being a problem.

When I'm fully experiencing my feelings, I enjoy the minutes and days I have with my girls as well as everything else going on in my life. I feel like I'm finally participating fully in my own life. When we take a walk, for example, I'm not thinking in the past or in the future. I just enjoy every word they say or every flower they notice. We make dinner together and enjoy the process from choosing our food to cleaning up. We go out on the deck and spend time under the stars with a huge bowl of popcorn. Finally, we grow sleepy in a big tangled heap of blankets and pillows, Dad, the dog, and the girls. Every single minute offers its own unique pleasure.

Because I'm focusing on the beauty of the moment, I am free to fully experience what I'm feeling. The minute I look for what's wrong or recall what we "have" to do, or look at what we don't have or why someone has screwed up, I'm simply not here enjoying my life. I'm stuck in that backward side of the energy circle.

The cost of not being able to feel fully is obvious. We stay stuck, we can't feel joy, we lose our aliveness. More and more researchers are finding that our physical health is directly related to our mental well-being. Our productivity dives, our creativity declines, and our self-esteem and ability to be at our best are diluted.

The benefits of feeling fully are clearly the flip side of the coin. We experience aliveness, creativity, self-esteem, better

"Every teacher I've consulted agrees
that the need for gangs would go away
if kids were only treated
with respect and dignity
and listened to at home—
if we saw their beauty
instead of their spots,
if we began to accept them
for who they are
and what they feel."

"The cost of not being able to feel fully is obvious.
We stay stuck, we can't feel joy,
we lose our aliveness.
Our productivity dives, our creativity declines,
and our self-esteem and
ability to be at our best are diluted.
The benefits of feeling fully
are clearly the flip side of the coin.
We experience aliveness, creativity,
self-esteem, better health,
and better coping skills."

health, and better coping skills to get us through the situations life does throw our way.

Every tool works beautifully to shape this gift.

When we experience our emotions fully, we're modeling who we really are as individuals. We let our children see it's OK to feel mad or sad or glad. They learn healthy, appropriate ways to deal with their feelings as they absorb how we act and react.

A lot of parents have asked in our seminars if they should work out their disagreements in front of the children. As we saw in the chapter on the Model Tool, how we live our lives becomes their blueprint for life. Where else would we like our children to learn how to resolve conflict? The other options so often portrayed in the popular media seem pretty grim to me—hitting, screaming, sulking, and pulling out a weapon are just a few I've seen in just the last few weeks and are certainly not what I want my daughters to emulate.

Forward focus questions like those we talked about with the Teach Tool, of course, are essential. "How do you feel about this? What do you think we should do? What would you like to do to change this?" Be prepared to move in small steps, though, if necessary. Sometimes feelings are so overwhelming, we need space just to feel them, get through them and process them before we're ready to talk.

Staying focused on the forward side of the energy circle sends the message that "You are all right. It's OK to be where you are, feeling what you feel."

> *This morning Emmy and Ali and I were rushing around to leave on time for a project we were working on out of town. The girls kept tormenting each other, fighting over clothes and who was going to wear what. Screams erupted from their room: "Get off my stuff!" "Don't let the dog take that." "I hate you."*
>
> *I listened to the brouhaha for a while and suddenly*

slipped back into my old pattern. "I can't stand this any-more," I yelled over their din. "Ali, you get out of here and go to my room." Suddenly, I stopped and caught myself. I left the room and went into the kitchen where I keep a framed poster of our "Pink Heart"—a heart illustrating the five parenting tools.

I realized the messages I was sending were pretty fright-ful: Among them, that they were bad kids, that conflict is wrong, they couldn't take care of themselves, they were a pain to be with, I didn't like them when they were like this, they couldn't handle their own problems, they were helpless and, worst of all, if they just escalate the uproar enough someone will always come flying in and solve their prob-lems.

I went back to their room and asked Ali to come back in. I said, "You guys play and work together so well ninety-nine percent of the time. In fact, it amazes me how well you treat each other and get along." I could see the messages register-ing as they started to shift.

"It's perfectly normal to have disagreements once in a while," I continued, "and I have all the faith in the world that you will figure out your problem and solve it just as you've done so often in the past. Let me know what you de-cide to do about it."

They were walking tall and proud when they came out for breakfast, loving each other again, and feeling good about solving the problem. Otherwise the next three hours would have been unbearable with their residual bickering and sniping.

(By the way, they decided to let Ali wear one of Emmy's shirts since Ali's were all dirty. You can be sure, however, that if I had suggested that answer it would not have been the right one.)

In any situation like this, if I were to backward-focus on how "bad" the feelings they had were or scold them for feeling that way, I would be superimposing my own definition and feelings about the situation rather than honoring what they're really feeling. The child gets labeled as an "angry" or "stupid" or "irresponsible" kid (which will be perpetuated since we go toward what we focus on), or the feeling becomes contrived just to get attention.

The Listen Tool is probably the biggest help of all for handling feelings. This means master listening—without emotionalism, interruptions, or "better ideas." It means loving, neutral listening, but not smothering listening. It also means not playing up the pain so the child gets credit for the pain, or being so emotional that the child gets fearful that this feeling will be too much to handle.

By using these tools to establish the foundation for emotionally healthy children, inappropriate behavior will diminish. The process will take time, though. We tiptoe around feelings so much in our society, some kids don't even know themselves what they are feeling. They may not trust themselves or their parents to open up and start sharing. Professional counseling is an extremely helpful and healthy way to open some channels between family members.

A number of parents who have participated in family counseling have found that using the tools in the "old" way only sabotaged the help they were getting. Using them the new way augmented the professional help and built new bridges they had only dreamed of before.

"Feelings, bless 'em, are to enjoy, not to analyze.
Watch a kid go bouncing down a yellow brick road,
then tell me how the whimsical 'why' in the smile
around his heart gets twisted into
the weary, worrisome, diagnostic
'why' of adulthood."

—Catherine Bauer, essayist

CHAPTER EIGHT

The Gift of Self-Esteem

It was a pretty ordinary moment. My daughters and I were enjoying a snack of fresh oranges. I noticed Emmy cut hers into two horizontal sections—like a grapefruit—instead of several vertical segments as I always did. She was enjoying that orange to the max, nibbling it around the edges, slurping from the center, squeezing the juice into her mouth.

I could have berated her for not eating it the "right" way (i.e., "my way"), or pointed out how it was easier for juice to drip on her the way she was eating it, or I could have just ignored it altogether. All of these responses were part of my old low-road parenting repertoire.

Instead, I took genuine delight in her creative attack on that orange. I told her I thought she had a really interesting idea. I asked her where she'd learned to cut it like that and would she show me how to do it too? I loved watching her

"If you don't feel good about yourself,
you'll just feel terrible all your life.
If you don't think you're good
at certain stuff, you're going to be bad at it.
When I feel good about myself,
I feel proud and happy."

—Rusty Borneman, age 8

"No matter how many of our children's teachers
or friends—or eventually, therapists—
acknowledge their value, our children's real
sense of self-worth initially comes from us,
their parents."

"When you know your children have
strong self-esteem you don't have to worry
about how to control their contact with others.
You can't really control it anyway.
But you can remind your children
of how wonderful they are
and how lucky those other kids will be
when your child's values rub off on them."

eyes light up and her self-esteem ratchet up another notch.
I'd noticed what she'd done. I asked her questions. I'd ac-
knowledged her creativity. I wanted to learn from her!

Could the possibility of a little dribble of orange juice on
her shirt ever compare with the gift of enhanced self-
esteem? My reaction to that ordinary event determined
which way Emmy would see the moment and either gain
from it or have a little more value chipped from her soul.

If I could give my child no other gift in the world, my top
choice would be self-esteem. Without it, we wither. With it, we
thrive.

Unfortunately, self-esteem doesn't come programmed in
our genes, we can't add any kind of magic elixir to our babies'
formula to start it growing. No matter how many of our children's teachers or friends—or eventually, therapists—acknowledge their value, our children's real sense of self-worth initially
comes from us, their parents.

Every moment of our lives augments or diminishes our self-
esteem: the responses we get from others, our interactions with
others, how we learned to treat ourselves from watching our
parents.

When you have high self-esteem you are nearly invincible.
No matter what happens, you still know that you are a good
and capable person, that you can do what you need to do again
and even better. You have a rich supply of inner strength. You
approach every moment, every event, every interaction with an
attitude of openness instead of fear, giving instead of taking, acknowledging your strengths rather than your weakness. You
see abundance and opportunity instead of shortage and trouble.

High self-esteem allows you to continue to validate and
nourish yourself on a regular basis. Self-esteem is apparent in
everything you do, from how you listen to new ideas and
whether you'll try something new, how you handle a conversa-

"It's so easy to pick out the children
who lack the gift of self-esteem.
They're the bullies on the playground,
the underachievers in school,
the kids who get taken advantage of.
They are our high-school dropouts,
the kids who can't say no to deadly drugs
or inappropriate sex
or a ride with a drunken driver
or an invitation to join a gang."

"When you give love messages, you're boosting
your child's self-worth.
When you focus on their strengths
rather than on their weaknesses,
their self-esteem can only rise.
When you teach through questions
rather than telling,
they find the world of their own creativity
and talent and abilities
they might otherwise never
have discovered or acknowledged."

tion, and how you see others to the very essence that people perceive as you.

As I work with both big and small companies on leadership development and training, it's often easy to see that the problems keeping these businesses from success are not obstacles imposed by "The Company." You know the usual complaints you hear from employees and bosses alike: This company is so rigid. . . . This company doesn't appreciate what we do every day. . . . These employees just don't want to work hard, the work ethic is dead. . . . The people here are so petty and jealous. . . . This company discriminates against (pick one) women, men, minorities, young people, old people, people with children, etc.

"Companies" can't do anything to anybody, but people sure can. Inevitably I find that the success of any business is in direct proportion to the kind of qualities and values and principles each employee holds and the culture the company creates to foster those qualities. Not only will healthy doses of self-esteem create a successful family, but you're also practically ensuring that your child will become a valued employee, no matter what he or she decides to do.

> *I'm very proud of my children, says Debbie. You always get what you expect. If you say your child's dumb or won't succeed, that's what you'll get. I have always tried to tell my children they're wonderful, that I'm very proud of them, that they can succeed at whatever they want.*
>
> *For example, my son Joe has always been a born leader. He has a quiet confidence that is quite infectious. One day, a strange woman came up to me and asked, "Are you Joe's mother? I want you to know that Joe is the most special, wonderful person and I just wanted to meet his mother."*

Joe may have been a "born leader," but it was definitely up to his parents to foster and nourish that quality appropriately or those leadership skills might have been used to bully or lead other kids into trouble.

Just think about when your children are exposed to other kids who may steal or drink or use drugs. When you know your children have strong self-esteem you don't have to worry about how to control their contact with others. You can't really control it anyway. But you can remind your children of how wonderful they are and how lucky those other kids will be when your child's values rub off on them.

> When picking her daughter up at school every day Marcia always asked Abby, "How did your day go? What's the best thing that happened to you today?"
>
> "I knew we had made great strides one day when she was in second grade when she said, 'The teacher gave me a sticker today. But you know what, Mommy, it doesn't matter if she gave me a sticker or not because I know I did a good job.' "
>
> "So much reinforcement in grade school is external, like stickers," Marcia explained. "But I want my child to have validation within herself. She connected that day and found her own validation even before the teacher gave her a sticker. She was responsible for her own 'feel good.' "

I know from my own life how important internal self-validation can be. When I was flying high with my talent agency, nothing could go wrong. I was strong, I was powerful, I was important. The day I lost that company I lost myself as well. I thought I was the company and my self-worth could only be as good as the business was. I could only function as long as other people admired me and flattered me. When left to do that on my own, I had no reserves to draw from.

It's so easy to pick out the children who lack the gift of self-esteem. They're the bullies on the playground, the underachievers in school, the kids who get taken advantage of. They are our high-school dropouts, the kids who can't say no to deadly drugs or inappropriate sex or a ride with a drunken driver or an invitation to join a gang. They're the grown-ups who miss out on career opportunities, who think they're not good enough, who have to belittle others to make themselves feel important, the ones who are always looking for other people's "spots." They're the parents who can't acknowledge their own or their children's greatness, thus perpetuating the cycle for generations.

Do you remember Deanna who we talked about in the Listen Tool chapter? She's the woman who was ignored by a mother whose sense of self died when her husband did.

Although Deanna has made vast strides in personal growth and repairing her own damaged self-esteem, her first two children are beginning to act out their own low self-esteem by skipping school and by not taking care of themselves. The pain in watching her children and grandchild suffer the effects of low self-esteem is intense.

The cycle of pain and dysfunction is continuing for her as it does for so many families unless they can break their old habits. Remember how each of the five tools we looked at in the earlier chapters has both an old and new way of using it? The old way usually got the job done; the new way not only gets the job done but leaves your child with valuable qualities to shape his or her life. Every one of the tools greatly enhances self-esteem.

When you really listen, when you catch a feeling, you validate the child and his or her own sense of reality. When you model your own self-esteem, your child sees how your life is enhanced, what power and control you have to make your own choices. When you give love messages, you're boosting the child's self-worth. When you focus on their strengths rather than on their weaknesses, their self-esteem can only rise. When you teach through questions rather than telling, they find the world of their own creativity and talent and abilities they might otherwise never have discovered or acknowledged.

A powerful sign in a hospital I visited one day said: "AIDS: 100 percent deadly, 100 percent preventable." Kids with high self-esteem know how to say "No" to dangerous situations; kids with low self-esteem look to anyone else to decide what's right for them. Or they don't see themselves as worthy of self-care. Which child would you like to have in these times when our children are constantly exposed to drugs, gangs, sexually transmitted diseases, and alcohol abuse?

More than any other gift, parents have told us they want their children to have the ability to make responsible decisions. Teachers tell us over and over again that they wish more than anything that children had more of this quality. They know from everyday experience with hundreds of different children how vital self-esteem is to peak performance, to learning, to setting and achieving goals.

This point was driven home forcibly during an outbreak of gang activity in Denver this year. Eric Poole, a criminal justice professor who had studied kids from the toughest neighborhoods, found some interesting conclusions. In those neighborhoods, whether a child joined a gang had almost nothing to do with the size of his family, the number of parents at home, their education or income. Rather, it had to do with whether the child had anyone in his life who would be disappointed if he joined a gang.

Poole also found that it took much greater character to resist a gang's influences than to succumb to them. Those who do resist seem to have a much stronger sense of who they are.

With a high level of self-esteem you know that you are a good and capable person no matter what happens. You know you can do whatever needs to be done again, and perhaps even better tomorrow. You approach every moment, every event, every interaction with an attitude of openness instead of fear, giving instead of taking, strength rather than weakness. You see abundance and opportunity instead of shortage and trouble.

What a magnificent gift!

"Whether you believe you can or you can't, you're right!"

—Henry Ford

"When I saw a baby bird on the ground,
I wanted to save it.
I tried hard, but it died anyway
and it made me cry."

"One time when my mom was real sick,
I rubbed her back, brought her juice,
and told her I loved her.
Is that what you mean by compassion?
I mean, that's a long word!"

—Rusty Borneman, age 8

CHAPTER NINE

The Gift of Compassion

I was having a really rough day. I was grouchy and self-ishly thinking of no one but myself while also wondering why everyone was so nasty to me. Emmy and Ali were pulling at my sleeves as we worked our way through gro-cery shopping, nagging me for pennies to ride the mechani-cal horse at the front of the store. I gave them a couple of pennies.

The horse was popular that day and the girls had to wait in line. I watched three-year-old Ali wait nearly ten min-utes while all the other kids and her sister took their turns. Finally it was hers. Instead of climbing on the horse, she went over to a little boy who was watching longingly and who she knew didn't have a penny. She put him up on the horse and gave him her ride.

Ali had wanted to ride the horse so desperately, and she had waited so patiently. Her simple act of compassion changed my entire day. "How can I be so selfish and crabby," I thought, "when that little girl just epitomized what this world should be like?"

Ali never told a soul that she did that and didn't know I was watching her. She never knew what a valuable gift she had given me as I watched her stand there with a loving smile on her face as the little boy rode on.

Compassion—the dictionary defines it as "sympathetic consciousness of others' distress together with a desire to alleviate it." I further define it as an essential component of being an effective, thriving inhabitant of this planet.

To me, being compassionate means coming from a special place in your heart and mind, appreciating and valuing everything and everyone's place in the grand scheme of life. I know that's difficult some days, so be compassionate with yourself, too, and acknowledge yourself for doing as well as you are.

I wrote in Chapter Seven about the gift of feeling fully. Our hearts can only be open and compassionate toward others when we have fully experienced ourselves.

Compassion, to me, means always walking in the other person's shoes, being considerate of their point of view whether or not you agree with it. My colleague Allison always includes "and to always give more than we take" in her definition of compassion.

The lack of compassion shows up in so many ways in today's world. I see kids who have no concern for where they throw their trash, how they treat school textbooks or materials from the public library. They crank up their boombox or car radio when people around them react in visible pain or anger to the offensive noise. They vandalize their school or church with no apparent regard for the consequences.

Hundreds of teachers have attended our "10 Greatest Gifts" seminars. Two Wyoming teachers, Pris and Linda, told us first, and we now hear it from teachers from all over the country: their biggest recurring problems at school come from children whose first reaction to a frustrating or confrontational situation is to lash out, to use their brawn instead of their brains.

" 'Conflict resolution' was never mentioned in all my years of college training," said one teacher, "but it's the primary issue I deal with all day long, far more than any academic subject I should be teaching."

I was reminded of this during an outbreak of youth violence and death in my own town. The community was outraged, but unfortunately not surprised when one young teen shot another in a confrontation unrelated to gangs in a nearby park. His mother had given him the gun. What kind of a message did that "gift" give that young man?

As the violence blazed on I watched dozens of parents lament their children's actions, parents who genuinely did not seem to know how their youngsters had come to such violent extremes, parents who wanted the cops or the community or someone to be responsible and stop "them." I wanted to cheer one night when I saw one mom from a particularly hard-hit neighborhood speak up at a televised meeting. "You want to know where the responsibility starts and ends?" she asked. She thumped her own chest emphatically as she asserted, "Right here, that's where."

Barb, an elementary-school principal, shared how exciting it is for her when she finally hears children reacting to taunting or bullying by saying things like, "I'm sorry, I won't do it again" instead of blaming the other kid, or "What did you want me to do that I didn't do?" or "How can I be friends with you?" Those are children who definitely have the gift of compassion!

In the business world I often see adults whose only concern is ever-increasing profits, no matter who they're stepping on— an employee, another business, the earth itself.

People like this, who seem to have grown up without the

"Being compassionate means coming from
a special place in your heart and mind,
appreciating and valuing
everything and everyone's place
in the grand scheme of life.
I know that's difficult some days
so be compassionate with yourself, too,
and acknowledge yourself
for doing as well as you are."

"You want to know where the responsibility
starts and ends?
Right here, that's where."

quality of compassion, fit a wonderful description I heard Texas governor Ann Richards use: "They grew up playing 'I Win, You Lose' instead of 'Let's All Play and Have Fun Together.' "

Does that mean we have to give up our cherished notion of "competitiveness" in business? That we shouldn't play to win? Not at all. However, I think the smartest businesses today are those that have a new definition of "winning." They no longer claw and kick their way to win at any cost, but instead make customers their highest priority. They listen to customers, care about them, and respond to their needs. They constantly strive for deeper levels of customer service and value.

The same thing is happening inside their companies. The old scenario had departments and employees competing against each other, vying for scarce resources. The attitude of successful companies is: How can we achieve our ultimate purpose in a way that's beneficial to all of us? How do we achieve our common mission of serving the customer instead of beating out the other guy?

I believe children are born with a natural sense of compassion which our behavior either enhances or eliminates as they grow up to emulate our example.

Compassion has many faces.

My girls each received $25 from their grandparents last Christmas. Both left their money lying in the kitchen where we had opened the mail, as they went rushing off to finish a project in the other room. I wondered aloud to them if our dog Wister might think the money was something tasty for him since he was confined to the kitchen and seemed to think anything lying around was a treat for him.

Emmy reacted by getting up and putting her money in her room. Ali went on with her project. Wister enjoyed his $25 dessert very much.

I listened and shared Ali's pain, but privately agonized

over the most compassionate way to deal with this. It would have been easy to reach into my pocket and replace the lost money. What seemed far better, however, was to let her experience the natural consequences of her inaction. Better a $25 lesson today—although that was a fortune to her—than a thousand-dollar lesson when she's older.

I remembered a college friend whose family gave her everything. If her dog had eaten $25 of hers, her family would have immediately replaced it and probably would have given her another $25 to ease her pain. Money not only filled all her physical needs; she grew up thinking it would fill all her emotional needs as well. She became heavily addicted to cocaine when she found she couldn't buy friends at college. Genuine love was not to be had for any price.

Another parent told me that, for him, compassion meant listening closely and with understanding to his sons when their new kitten died. Their pain was doubled when their mother, with whom they lived during the week, kept saying that it was only a cat, and it could be replaced easily.

I wondered about the messages those boys were getting. I wondered if maybe those young minds worried that no one would miss them if they died. Maybe their mom would simply go down to the pound and pick up a couple of new kids. In any event, their genuine feelings of pain for a living creature were totally discounted.

Their dad went to the Humane Society with the boys when they were ready to adopt a new cat. He asked lots of questions about what they needed to do to take care of an animal and how long they needed to be responsible for it. In addition to using the Teach Tool, he was also focusing forward on the caring and love our pets need. I know this dad will also include lots of love messages when he notices the boys taking care of the animals at his house or hears them talking about the cat at their mom's house.

> One day the girls and I were in the checkout line at a grocery store where the cashier was surly and rude. The girls innocently asked him how he was doing. He responded angrily, accusing them of staring at him and making him feel uncomfortable. They were stunned at his response.
>
> As we left the store, we talked about his reaction. The girls demonstrated true compassion. We noted that the clerk had an extremely poor complexion and was probably very sensitive about it. It was a hot, sticky day and many customers were probably reacting rudely as well. The girls realized that they were not bad but that they had to allow this man to work through his own apparent pain, because there was no way they could know what he might be feeling at that moment.

I see my girls responding to the everyday ways I try to demonstrate compassion. We recycle everything to help the earth. They ask which financially strapped family we'll choose to take Christmas gifts to this year. There are a number of older people in our neighborhood whose only social interaction for days may be the people who talk to them as they walk past their house. The girls now join me to chat when we meet them on the sidewalk.

These girls are definitely coming from their hearts as they "walk in other people's shoes."

The poem on the next page speaks clearly of compassion, no matter what your choice of spiritual path.

THE WORK OF CHRISTMAS

When the song of the angels is stilled,
When the star in the sky is gone,
When the kings and princes are home,
When the shepherds are back with their flock,
The work of Christmas begins:

To find the lost,
To heal the broken,
To feed the hungry,
To release the prisoner,
To rebuild the nations,
To bring peace among others,
To make music in the heart.

From "The Work of Christmas," by Howard Thurman.
© 1973 Howard Thurman.
Reprinted with permission.

"When my life isn't in balance,
I get bored, restless, and angry at other people.
I feel good and happy and organized
when my life is in balance."

—Lindy Kedro, age 13

"When I feel stressed out, and out of balance,
I take my feelings out on my mom.
I feel like I'm on an emotional roller-coaster."

—Casey Lebsack, age 14

CHAPTER TEN

The Gift of Balance

- *My life's out of balance. I can't catch up. It's a constant juggling act.*
- *On the teeter-totter of life, I'm always down, it seems.*
- *My life's gone flat line—I'm neither up nor down, sad nor glad, laughing nor crying; it's just another blur of a day.*
- *Help, I'm spinning out of control.*
- *Daddy, I'm bored—there's nothing to do.*
- *(For weeks before Christmas): Oh boy, I can hardly wait for Christmas. I wonder what I'm going to get. This is so exciting. . . . (An hour after the presents are opened): What a drag. Is this all there is? How come Jamie's presents are better than mine?*

Ever hear anything like this from your kids, your friends, your spouse, yourself?

Whenever I hear these kinds of statements, I see someone

out of balance. Unfortunately, I find so many kids and adults who missed out on the gift of balance in their life—and who are paying the price of imbalance now.

I know the cost—I'm one of those people. My problem with balance is that I think I have to work all the time or I have no value. I want to have my friends know how hard I'm working so they'll think I'm good and virtuous.

When I'm out of balance, my work becomes my identity. I lose my uniqueness, because everything depends on how my day went. I stop working for joy, for making a difference, for helping people; my life becomes just work, a big to-do list.

When I'm not in balance I tend to be unhappy and I tend to go toward the back side of the energy circle. I'm fearful, focused on problems and the reasons things can't be done. My energy's gone, as are creative thinking and clarity of thought. I can't do either me or the world any good.

And, remember, since we go toward what we focus on, I'm assured of getting more of whatever I'm concentrating on: more problems, more fear, more things that don't get done.

I grew up hearing life is not supposed to be easy, it's supposed to be a struggle. We have to work hard all the time. And yet, a life of work without time for play, for spiritual fulfillment, for time to just be—in other words, a life without a healthy mix of stillness and action, work and play, thinking and doing—will indeed be a life of drudgery.

In my career, when I have the discipline to stay balanced, my work is refreshing, energetic, creative, focused, passionate. When I don't stay balanced, no matter how hard I work, I can't even appreciate the results. It's a long, hard journey with no apparent destination.

And so, as I learn more and more each day to create balance in my life, I realize what an incredibly valuable gift it is to my children as well. We're working on it together.

I want to set a model of balance—emotional, physical, spiritual, and intellectual balance. I want them to know that the journey of life includes both pain and joy, work and play. Each one teaches you about the other. They all keep a life healthy and productive.

When I'm feeling balanced, no matter what I'm doing, I can't think of anything else I'd rather do. When I'm not in balance, everything becomes a chore, another job to get done, another day to get through.

Balance is necessary in everything in life. I see it in myself after I've been with my kids for a week and I'm on the way home from the town where their mother lives. I miss them so much it hurts, but I wouldn't feel the pain if I hadn't known the joy of being with them.

One example of an out-of-balance child is an overorganized child. His harried parents are pushed to the wall managing his activities and transporting him from one place to the next. They live an "If it's Tuesday, this must be a soccer field" existence. The children are continually scheduled for dance lessons, music lessons, karate lessons. Or sports practice, Girl Scouts, church programs. Or kids' day at the museum, skating, acting, or swimming groups. Add the pressures of being a single parent or having several children and life gets even more complex and stressful.

I have nothing against organized kids' activities. It beats having them hang around the mall or on the street corner all day doing nothing. I object when our children are so organized that they lose the gift of spontaneity, when they think nothing can happen until adults are around to provide them with form and structure.

These are the kids who drive us to tightly gritted teeth when we hear one more time, "I'm bored, there's nothing to do," as they sit around waiting for adults to structure their lives or sup-

"In my career, when I have the discipline to stay
balanced, my work is refreshing, energetic,
creative, focused, passionate.
When I don't stay balanced,
no matter how hard I work,
I can't even appreciate the results.
It's a long, hard journey with no
apparent destination."

"I want them to know that the journey of life
includes both pain and joy, work and play.
Each one teaches you
about the other. They all keep a life
healthy and productive."

ply their entertainment. Or they may be the children who sit around staring at the TV or constantly playing video games. They lack a vital balance of spontaneity versus organized events, of time for reflection, of self-directed activities, of simply enjoying the process of savoring the moment or smelling the roses.

They've become as obsessed with activities as many adults are with work.

When is it that our children move from that glorious "Oh, boy, guess what I *get* to do today?" to that soul-numbing "Oh, man, guess what I *have* to do today?"

I see employees in all kinds of industries who simply wait around to be told what to do next. As children, their time was always managed for them, they were told what they ought to do and how they ought to do it, so they wait for the same kind of direction from a boss. And they wonder why they resent their jobs so much.

Or I watch the young people who flounder through the first few weeks or months, or sometimes even years of college, because they've never learned to manage their own time, make their own decisions, keep a healthy balance of work and play, rest and activity, quiet time and social events.

I really want to help my girls stay off the rigid, narrow pathway of imbalance. I'd like them to see that it's OK to just sit and think, to enjoy quiet times. That it's OK to be on a project and work all night and not be hung up on a rigid schedule. That it's OK for us to be sad or glad on any given day. I want them to know they need to think for themselves.

Finally, I want them to see that each piece of life—whether it be physical, mental, or spiritual—is part of the whole tapestry.

One of the best tools for giving the gift of balance is modeling. As our children see where our priorities are, they reflect that balance in their own lives. Balance truly is one of the gifts

"When is it that our children move
from that glorious 'Oh, boy, guess what I
get to do today?' to that soul-numbing
'Oh, man, guess what I have to do today?' "

"Ali had reminded me of the need
to simply let go now and then;
that on life's priority list, people and dogs
are far more important than chores."

"We are all on the journey to mastery.
There are times when we're apparently
stuck on a plateau;
sometimes we're flying high.
I want my children to know
that life is a journey
and there are all kinds of times
along the way."

kids don't get from a lecture; they only can see it from how we live our lives over the years and what the results are.

> I was too busy ironing clothes one day to pay attention to my dog, Mister Wister, who was whining for attention and generally being a nuisance. My seven-year-old noticed, however, and asked me: "Dad, what's most important right now, ironing or taking Wister for a walk?"
>
> Well, no contest. The ironing could easily wait until another time. But more important, Ali had reminded me of the need to simply let go now and then; that on life's priority list, people and dogs are far more important than chores.

Ali helped me reach this point, but the results are what's keeping me here. When I take time to stay in balance, to refresh myself with play, I get so much more work done when I return to it.

How important is it to listen to how our children are feeling and to honor those feelings, no matter where they fall on the pleasure/pain spectrum?

How many of you have had to deal with children who are almost out of control with rage or disappointment when their team loses the big tournament? Or when they didn't get what they wanted for their birthday? Or you don't have the resources to get them something they think they absolutely can't live without? These are times when they are clearly out of balance as that thing or that win becomes so all-consuming that it blocks everything else out of their lives.

Listening helps our children get a sense of perspective and balance. We need to truly listen—no lectures, no advice, no judgments. As we listen, we validate their feelings and let them pour out their rage or sadness or terror. You already know what often happens if a child has to stuff his or her feelings. You suffer for hours or even days with a grumpy, uncooperative, door-slamming bundle of unhappiness.

Have you ever noticed a family whose child is having a screaming tantrum? They try ignoring the child, screaming at him, dragging him along, even hitting him. What's the message to the child? "You shouldn't have that feeling, it's bad, we don't care what you're feeling, stuff it!" More often than not, I've found that parents who stop, listen, listen, and listen some more, not only find the tears and screams subside, but also leave the child with the invaluable gift of knowing it's OK to have bad feelings, that you don't have to act out on them, and there are always choices to working out a problem situation.

First and foremost, our children simply need someone to listen. A celebrity who recently lost her daughter in an accident recalled how everyone was tremendously sympathetic, but that they all had some little piece of advice. "That really ticked me off," she said. "I really just wanted them to listen to my pain."

We can use the Focus Tool to move ourselves or our family to the forward side of the energy circle. One day recently, I couldn't see my desk for all the work piled on it. I was running scared about all the work I had to do and how I couldn't possibly get it done. I could have stayed stuck on that back side of the circle, focusing on my problems, how I wasn't good enough, and wondering who I could blame for this mess.

Instead, I asked myself what I had accomplished so far that day. I was astounded at how much I had done. I congratulated myself for getting so much done and rewarded myself with some play time. I came back refreshed, balanced, and in a much better space to make decisions that propelled me forward to the solutions I wanted.

I had the luxury of being self-employed then so I could leave my work behind for a few minutes. Can you change your focus in the midst of babies crying, dinner boiling over and the phone ringing off the hook? Admittedly, it's a lot harder, but here's what some people I know do.

A single father tells me he hums. "Humming changes my

vibrations or something," he says. "Maybe it's because it makes me breathe deeper. If I can get the kids to join in, we usually end up giggling uncontrollably and somehow the moment seems brighter."

Another parent told me she simply stops to survey the situation and wonders how Erma Bombeck would write about it or what it would look like in her favorite family comic strip. "It doesn't magically clean the stove or change the baby, but it nudges me off the problem and onto the solution."

And messages, of course, play a big role in acknowledging and celebrating our children when they are living in balance. Notice when your child is doing what keeps her in balance in her own life and, of course, she'll try harder to do more. I love to acknowledge Emmy for her ability to play intensely with her friends one minute and be curled up in a corner doing her homework the next.

The Teach Tool can be particularly effective. Recently, I was caught up in some business matters and barely even acknowledged the girls' existence as I whirled from one activity to another. I woke up—literally—the next morning to realize how out of balance I was.

I asked the girls what they had noticed about how frantic I'd been the night before. "How effective was that?" I asked. "What did that do to our evening together? What did you feel like when someone so fixated on a project was around you or when you got overextended with activities? Would you like to know what being so out of balance did to me?"

When they accepted that "invitation to learn," I was able to communicate to them how ineffective I'd felt the night before, how it had taken me four hours to get something done that normally would have taken only an hour or less. I told them I'd gotten a headache then and I was tired now. Most of all I didn't allow myself time to have fun with them.

I could have lectured them for a week on the need for balance in our lives, but the questions helped them internalize and own the answers immediately.

We are all on the journey to mastery. There are times when we're apparently stuck on a plateau; sometimes we're flying high. I want my children to know that life is a journey and there are all kinds of times along the way. It's OK to just be where you are, but the path is infinitely richer when it is full of all kinds of experiences—work and play, pleasure and pain—and our lives flow when we are in balance.

"Balance—the key to peace and wisdom."

—Azura, writer/lecturer

"The mind ought sometimes to be diverted that it may return the better to thinking."

—Phaedrus

"When I'm laughing and having a great time,
it feels like my jaw is made out of steel
and my mouth can't close because I'm laughing
so hard. It feels like my cheeks are getting blown up
like balloons and they're going to pop."

—Emily Vannoy, age 9

"Sometimes I can't breathe when I'm laughing so hard.
And when I'm having that much fun
it feels like there's a big fire on my heart."

—Alison Vannoy, age 7

CHAPTER ELEVEN

The Gift of Humor

I was admiring new kittens at a friend's house the other day. "Are they boy cats or girl cats?" I asked my friend's three-year-old daughter.

"I don't know," she said as she picked them up and turned them over. "Mom always looks to see what's stamped on the bottom."

Ah, the gift of humor. Not teasing, not taunting someone because they're different or less powerful, but a genuine expression of joy at the pleasures and ironies and foibles of life. Laughter not only renews our souls; medical researchers are finding it restores our body's health as well.

It was one of those terrible days for Yancey, at home with her sons Casey and Ward, then ages three and four. There was a solid downpour, way too nasty for the kids to play outside. By the time they'd finished squeezing toothpaste into the electrical outlets in the bathroom, she was scream- ing, "Why can't you kids learn to be good and stay out of trouble?" Casey, by then tap dancing in the toilet with his good shoes on, called back: "Mom, we're little. We're trying to be good, but we just haven't learned how yet."

Without a sense of humor, life can be colorless, a terrible burden. With it, we enjoy the process of living. We have more joy to share with others. And we might even live longer with less stress and health problems. As Sarah, an elementary-school principal, says while standing in the midst of the apparent chaos of 450 little energy systems charging by, "Humor is the only thing that gives me objectivity."

"Why does that sign say we have to wait for the hostess to be seated?" queried five-year-old Jill in a restaurant. "Aren't we the ones that are going to be seated?"

Kids who grow up without a sense of humor live perpetu- ally in a state of fear and defensiveness. Their self-esteem col- lapses in their fear of being wrong. For years I couldn't laugh at myself because I was always worrying about what people thought about me. What they probably ended up thinking was that I must be some kind of humorless, uptight jerk.

The daughter of a friend of mine recently noticed a "Lost Our Lease" sign in a store window. "Why don't they just look for it?" she wondered.

People who have a strong sense of humor display joy and trust. They're usually good communicators because they can see all sides of an issue and know that making a mistake is not fatal. They usually have a lot of friends because they're exciting and stimulating to be with.

> *Scott was about four when Elvis Presley died. That week in Sunday School, the teacher asked who the first person on earth was. Scott waved his hand frantically. "Who do you think it was, Scott?" the teacher asked. "Elvis Presley," he answered confidently.*

The simplest things can crack us up around my house, and humor helps keep us objective and the day in perspective. We laugh around the office all the time and it results in much higher creativity and productivity. The clients feel the energy and respond positively.

> *I asked Jeremy when he was not quite three if he wanted a piece of cheese for lunch. "No," he said, "I want peace and quiet."*

Sometimes a humorous moment is just the right finishing touch for what might have been an otherwise stressful day. I was lying on the floor one night watching a movie on TV. Ali had lain down next to me and put her head on my shoulder. Just as Emmy was heading over to claim her spot on my other shoulder, our big black Labrador eyed the same spot and streaked across the room like a Stealth Jet from nowhere to claim the space first. By the time Emmy arrived—probably a full one and a half seconds later—Mister Wister seemed so deeply asleep he couldn't be roused or moved.

> *I asked three-year-old Leah if she'd like a grilled cheese sandwich. "No," she replied, "but could you make me a boy cheese sandwich?"*

"Without a sense of humor, life can be
colorless, a terrible burden.
With it, we enjoy the process of living.
We have more joy to share with others.
And we might even live longer
with less stress and health problems."

"Another healthy benefit of living a life
of fun and joy is learning the importance
of hugging and touching,
of nurturing one another
just by being together."

Another healthy benefit of living a life of fun and joy is learning the importance of hugging and touching, of nurturing one another just by being together.

The girls love it when I sit in our favorite big soft chair. One will come sit in my lap. The other one tiptoes up, pulls her sister gently off, drags her across the carpet, and then races back to climb into my lap ahead of the other. The first one careens back across the room, pulls her sister off . . . and the game goes on until we're on the floor hugging and giggling.

> *Ali came home from kindergarten one day after her teacher had been talking about the human race. "Daddy," she asked, "where's the human race? Can we go watch it?"*

Humor is really a tool for life itself, and all five parenting tools help develop it. Of course, the way we model our own approach to life will leave our kids either making lemonade when life hands them lemons or, conversely, always trying to fix the blame instead of the problem.

The Listen Tool has us listen (yes, even though it's for the 43rd time) with interest and appropriate laughter to one more "Knock, knock. Who's there? Mickey Mouse's underwear." Or "Guess what? Chicken butt. Guess when? Chicken skin. Guess why? Chicken thigh."

> *Two-year-old Zach sat alone on the front stoop for a long while one evening. When he came back into the house he asked, "Can you see the starshine in my hair?"*

Our love messages acknowledge our children's efforts to develop their sense of humor. But it saddens me to see adults who use teasing as a way to interact with children, often, I think, because they're not comfortable dealing with real feelings with children. Teasing allows us to hide feelings behind a barrier of hurtful humor. And unfortunately, teasing or any humor that has a hurt message can so easily wipe out a child's fragile self-esteem.

Just as forward focus questions and FACing are primary ways of staying on the forward side of the circle, so is humor. The lighthearted approach is a great way to use the Focus Tool. We can FAC the kids when they use humor appropriately or when they look at the lighthearted side of a situation as well as the grim side. When I'm not on the forward side of the energy circle I can't see a jot of humor anywhere because I'm in fear, wondering what's wrong with me, what I have to do, what's not working well. There is no humor on the back side of the energy circle. Love and laughter and life all live on the forward side.

Oliver Wendell Holmes once observed, "Pretty much all the honest truth-telling there is in the world is done by children." Being a grandfather, and elementary school teacher for 32 years, I certainly agree. Here are some delightfully original observations about grandparents by their grandchildren:

"Grandmother's Easter dress was beautiful. It even had a hat that rhymed."

"She makes me stay indoors when it rains, but she lets me go outside as soon as the mud tightens up."

"The two unusual things about Granddad are the way he sleeps out loud and his hair is wearing out."

"Grandparents are one of the best by-products of family living."

"My grandparents can do wonderful things. Like they can put a twig of one tree on to the root of another tree and still have it grow. I will always put both gladness and wonder in my same thought about grandparents."

(Reprinted with permission from "Speaking of Grandparents" by Harold Dunn, SENIOR WIRE news syndication, Denver, Colorado, 1993.)

"Mirth is the sweet wine of human life. It should be offered sparkling with zestful life unto God."

—Henry Ward Beecher

"Good communication means sharing your feelings
and not holding them inside.
It means you speak clearly and slowly
so other people can hear you.
It means that you have fun talking."

—Emily Vannoy, age 9

"Good communication means you should not
copy another person's work.
And you shouldn't put other people down."

—Alison Vannoy, age 7

CHAPTER TWELVE

The Gift of Communication

He's a really nice guy, but he just can't communicate. ... She's a terrible boss, she just can't communicate. ... He's a terrific husband but he never tells me what's bothering him. ... I have no idea what my teenager thinks, she never tells me anything. ... I just can't get through to my husband why this is so important. ...

You get the idea.

The gift of communication is not only a set of reading and writing skills, but also an attitude of listening and understanding, of honoring the communicator for his or her thoughts and attitudes and ideas.

Without the gift of communication, our children have no way to express their natural creativity and imagination. Worse yet, they can never really hear what others are saying to them.

They resort to whining or complaining or fighting because no one seems to hear them.

With the gift of communication they can express their own ideas as well as hear different ideas from others. They can express feelings as easily as facts. Their sphere of influence in the world has almost no limits. And in the practical world, it is probably the most essential business skill they will ever learn. It is a gift of enormous potential.

> *As a child, I had so many chores at home on the farm, I had no time to get involved in school activities. Other kids joined the Future Farmers of America or the Key Club, but I was too busy at home. I didn't talk to anyone very much, and with no practice, I had no confidence in my skill to communicate. When I did have a few words to say, I didn't have the confidence to try it. Other times I had confidence but no communication skills. It was an endless cycle of frustration.*
>
> *Fast forward to 1969. Speech 101 at college. I couldn't sleep for a week before I had to do a simple five-minute talk. I would sit paralyzed with fear in all my classes and at every meeting, panicked that I might be called on. Sadly, I knew the answer but no one would ever know because I so dreaded having to say it.*
>
> *On to 1979. I'm sitting in a Chamber of Commerce meeting sprinkled with a lot of high-powered movers and shakers. I really wanted to make a difference in our community. My head was swimming with ideas on how to create the team, how to manifest effective solutions, but I was still paralyzed and unable to communicate my ideas.*

I couldn't seem to go out and get my ideas across except in one-on-one situations, and even that was very hard. It made everything I did twice as tough. I'd have ideas, feelings, I'd know the way things could get done, but I couldn't say them, I couldn't communicate them.

During the early days of my career, I had tremendous motivation, indelible commitment, high creativity—but I didn't have the piece of mental software to communicate to others. It was so painful, and it limited my ability to do good, to influence others, even to talk to others about ordinary events.

Learning to communicate well actually helps our children learn to think. A friend of mine will say something profound and then drop her mouth open in amazement. "I had no idea that's what I thought until I just said it."

Learning to write well is also an important part of good communication. While writing means paying attention to grammar and spelling, sentence structure and the flow of ideas, written pieces allow our kids to go back over what they've said to see if they have moved logically from one point to another. They get to evaluate what they actually think.

I'm astounded to *see* what I've just *said* to someone over the phone. My associate, Donna, and I will laugh hysterically when I read: "It was a pleasure to talk to you again at Susan and I's 25th reunion" or "We look forward to enhancing your enhancement of the corporate culture." Thank goodness, writing gives us a second, third, and even fourth chance to think about what we're trying to communicate.

On the other hand, we've all met people who babble on, creating a lot of verbal sound and fury signifying nothing. Simply speaking doesn't always mean there's thinking behind it.

Donna wraps up succinctly what good communication can mean for a family.

When I truly listen to someone it makes me feel as though I am so much more a part of that person. When my kids are communicating something important and I listen with full attention, it becomes a two-way dialog. If they are

"Good communication opens up so many doors:
good communicators get job interviews,
they develop great friendships and relationships
because they can both speak and listen
from the heart."

sharing vital information with me and I'm only half-present, it really isn't an exchange. In order for communication to happen there have to be a sender and a receiver. That's when we truly connect!

Good communication opens up so many doors: good communicators get job interviews, they develop great friendships and relationships because they can both speak and listen from the heart. Many people know what's really important to help other people, but if they can't communicate, their realm of influence is very small.

Good communication is crucial in today's business world, where you must be able to express ideas and motivate other people. What I often find keeps people from being promoted is that they can't communicate. At a recent conference of school administrators, I heard the staggering statistic that only 20 percent of our high school graduates have entry level career communication skills.

When we were interviewing for a new director of a department at Vannoy Talent, we talked to dozens of qualified applicants with outstanding references and commitment to our company's goals. All else being equal, we hired Carol, who was really strong in expressing and communicating her ideas. She could captivate a room with her energy and excitement. She used exciting words and honored everybody's else's thoughts as important too. Her career thrived with us.

The only way I learned communication skills was through practice. I practice all the time now with my children. We sing and speak on a tape recorder, we read out loud, share ideas verbally and in notes, we get involved in drama, and talk in front of groups.

I ask the girls dozens of questions so they have to think. I model speaking clearly on the tape recorder and into the telephone. I want to make sure my kids have all the pieces of the

"You could earn a Ph.D. in listening
but you still won't be a good listener
if you don't want to listen."

"Top leaders strive to garner commitment
from their people,
not just compliance."

"Good communication also means
that we don't say things
that belittle people.
It means being aware of other people's
needs and honoring where they are
and what they feel."

communication package—good pronunciation, breath control, well-thought-out ideas, and coherent presentation. We also focus on the other vital parts of good communication—listening, and the ability to share and to motivate.

And most important of all is attitude. Businesses can have the greatest tool package in the world and still fail miserably. Programs like Total Quality Management (TQM), and all the skill-based approaches like conflict resolution skills, negotiation skills, or communication or listening or brainstorming skills, are useless without the addition of attitude or state of mind. It's the "want to" part, the desire to apply what they know and to sincerely contribute to the success of the organization.

> *A buddy of mine was dropping off newspapers to be recycled at the grocery store. He noticed that an employee there didn't want to help either him or an older woman who was struggling to get her bundles of recyclable materials out of her trunk. The employee just kept playing football in the parking lot, completely ignoring the customers.*
>
> *My friend knew that if he complained to the management, by 7 the next morning there'd be a new employee rule about no footballs in the parking lot, plus another reminding workers that they were to snap to attention immediately whenever anyone opened their trunk.*

If the employees actually wanted to give greater quality and greater service, they would already know how to do it. There wouldn't have to be rules about no footballs in the parking lot or an edict to always help people unload their trunks. Every employee there could easily come up with three additional ways they could give better service.

You can earn a Ph.D. in listening but you still won't be a good listener if you don't *want* to listen. The intent and the "want to" are equally as important as the skill.

Top leaders strive to garner commitment from their people, not just compliance. The key that works in businesses—and in our homes—is to use communication skills like forward focus questions and careful listening so that each person develops the mind shift to form his or her own solutions, owns the responsibility to do things right, and develops the commitment to work at his or her highest level.

Good communication also means that we don't say things that belittle people. It means being aware of other people's needs and honoring where they are and what they feel. All five of the parenting tools enhance communication, especially the Focus Tool. If, from the back side of the energy circle, we're always looking for someone's fatal flaw, or what's wrong with the situation or the people in it, or what I'm upset about or what I don't like about what someone's saying, no real communication can ever happen. Such people can't listen because they're too busy defending themselves from your attack.

But when we're on the forward side of the energy circle, successful communication is nearly guaranteed because we're all working toward the same goal.

I've always wanted to communicate more with my papa. He is one of the most intelligent, wise people I've ever known. There's so much more I can learn from him, but when he's on the back side of the energy circle, being critical of everything, communication shuts down. I simply bow out. It's too painful to talk with him. Everybody loses.

The times when he is focusing forward and we can share ideas and solutions, communication opens up like a flower. There's an incredible difference.

Remember Hank and Nancy, who had the surly teenage daughter? The number-one thing they did to rebuild communication with her was to start noticing her "beauty." All they had done for years was focus on her "spots"—what they didn't like about her or her behavior or how she dressed or wore her hair or talked on the phone or didn't do her work.

A teacher named Jim called us a couple of weeks after the seminar he attended.

> *I can't believe the difference. I used to always ask my kids how their day was, what had happened that day. The results were zilch, no conversation, no information. At best, they'd say "Fine" and be gone. The difference when I switched to forward focus questions was extraordinary. Now I ask, "What's the best thing that happened today?" I can't get them to stop talking, not that I would ever want to. I've found out they lead some pretty interesting lives.*
>
> *And since I now know they go toward what they focus on, I realize they're always looking forward to the good things that happen. I only wish every family in America did this. I could take my students so much further if children were used to this kind of focus and communication at home.*

Finally, communication also means knowing that you can always ask for what you want, as well as offer help to others. Mary found her own life incredibly enhanced when her child was able to do that.

> *One thing I've always taught my son is that it's OK to ask for what you want. Your best chance of getting it, I'd remind him, is if you ask. Asking doesn't guarantee you'll get it, but go ahead and take the risk of asking for it.*
>
> *From the time he was in sixth grade through high school, he lived with his dad on the East Coast, halfway across the country, during the school year. One Christmas vacation I could tell something was on his mind. He finally took a deep breath and asked if he could come visit me on spring*

break instead of waiting until summer. He was always really glum about going back after Christmas vacation.

"Of course you can," I said. "We'll work out the expenses somehow. I'm delighted to be able to see you." He was so relieved and lighthearted after that. After going back to the East Coast, he called me and said he was so glad he had asked.

It was the first time I didn't cry after Christmas vacation because I know I would see him again soon.

"Talking and eloquence are not the same: to speak,
and to speak well, are two things.
A fool may talk, but a wise man speaks."

—Ben Jonson

"Thought is the blossom;
language the bud;
action the fruit behind it."

—Ralph Waldo Emerson

"Abundance is an extra bowl of ice cream
and getting to stay up late
and laughing a lot."

—Alison Vannoy, age 7

"Abundance means I have as many books
as I want to read and lots of warm clothes
for the wintertime.
And it means there's always lots of love."

—Emily Vannoy, age 10

"Abundance means we have everything we need
even though we don't have everything we want yet.
It makes me feel safe."

—Brian Cohen, age 14

CHAPTER THIRTEEN

The Gift of Abundance

I remember the phone call. Vannoy Talent had won a hard-fought battle that finally landed our first contract for a Cosmopolitan *cover girl. It was near quitting time and I was exhausted.*

The doubts began as I headed down the elevator. No sooner had I gotten my key in the ignition of my car than I was overwhelmed with fear. My mind was racing with questions like: "Can we do it again? What if they cancel the contract at the last minute? What about that Twentieth Century Fox job? Does my staff appreciate this success? Is that new agent going to work out?"

I couldn't take even a moment to enjoy this phenomenal victory.

Looking back over that period of my life, I realize I achieved incredible successes but I was never able to enjoy them. There was one major ingredient missing in my life—a strong sense of abundance.

The gift of abundance is what I consider the key to all the other qualities and values that make our lives and our children's lives so fulfilling. It allows us to view the world as a place of endless choices, endless opportunities, endless chances, endless growth. There is always another day and another way. It's a way of approaching the world in degrees of strength, instead of degrees of weakness, of living with degrees of love and goodness instead of degrees of fear.

I am enormously grateful to my parents for this gift. It has been an incredible advantage to me all my life, especially in business. If one deal doesn't work out, I know another one will. When I remember there is abundance in this world I can leave what looks like a losing situation and ask myself, "What can I learn from this?" and "What kind of value can we all receive from this?" If I forget to focus on abundance I bombard myself with questions like, "Now what's going to happen? How did I mess up?"

When I drift away from this concept the whole world suddenly flip-flops from bright to dark, from enthusiasm to lethargy, from optimism to fear.

Last fall a friend and I were driving down a beautiful mountain canyon. As a passenger I was free to take in the sights and sounds. For a half-hour I was completely overwhelmed by the endless shapes, sizes, textures and colors of the trees, rocks, bushes, streams, the sky. Driving up the canyon, I'd been absorbed in some deal I had to face that week, wondering if it would work out. But coming down, I simply let myself absorb and acknowledge the universe's endless abundance. It's always there but I don't always tune into it. When I do remember, I realize that everything in my life has this same unlimited abundance.

In my family it means we have endless opportunities for fun, humor, nurturing better qualities and values, a deeper level of enjoyment of all of our current and past activities, and always, always another chance.

> *Following a long, hot, tiresome day in the car a few years ago, the girls and I finally arrived at the Great Sand Dunes National Monument. They were cranky and definitely unhappy about seeing vast amounts of "boring" sand with nary a McDonald's or anything else in sight. My initial "old" response to their complaining would have been something like "This is a family vacation, dammit, so shut up and enjoy it."*
>
> *Instead I asked a lot of forward focus questions. What's different here than other places we've been? What do you think people do to have fun here? What could we do to have fun here if you could create any game you wanted to as long as it was safe? Pretty soon we were whooping it up in a spirited game of tag, rolling down the dunes, throwing sand to see where the wind would take it, and generally having a riotously good time. It's all a matter of where you focus your energy.*

I am truly amazed as I watch the children next door and their single mom manifest abundance in such creative ways.

Without the means to buy a lot of fancy toys, Juliette simply makes available a lot of ordinary items and the kids' imagination takes over. A set of skateboard wheels, old wood, and a milk crate became a truck, a go cart, a space ship. When string didn't work, six-year-old Adrian found bungee cords from their camping equipment that would.

The picnic bench is used to sit on, crawl under, or combine with the ladder from the swing set and some blankets and

"When I remember there is abundance
in this world I can leave what looks
like a losing situation and ask myself,
'What can I learn from this?' and
'What kind of value can we all receive from this?' "

"In my family it means we have endless
opportunities for fun, humor,
nurturing better qualities and values,
a deeper level of enjoyment of all of
our current and past activities,
and always, always another chance."

"It's so empowering to listen to all their ideas
while constantly giving love messages
to reinforce that there is always
another time, another way, another day."

sheets for a clubhouse. Boxes become a private room, a storage area, a maze, and more. Four-year-old Rika did his part for the environment by picking up all the spent fireworks in the neighborhood after the Fourth of July, but rather than throw them away, he made a fascinating sculpture for his bedroom.

One day, the kids wanted to have "brunch in Paris." They put the hose through the hole that drains the plastic swimming pool and attached a fan-shaped sprinkler to it. They put the picnic table near their "fountain" complete with an umbrella in a big bottle to steady it. They added a pot of flowers, made some scrambled eggs—and voilà! They had their brunch in Paris!

What a contrast to the children who whine and beg their parents that they must have more and more new toys, many times because they lack the gift of abundance—and the creativity and imagination that spring from it.

Let me tell you the story of two young people and their new bikes.

Tiffany had a nice bicycle but decided that she absolutely had to have a new one, like her friends. She made her parents so uncomfortable with her whining and pleading that they took her out last weekend and bought the new one she wanted. Tiffany doesn't have the foggiest idea how much it cost but she knows she got what she wanted.

I used to think I was doing my kids such a great favor by giving them a gift, but this next mom used the five tools to give her son a bundle of wonderful free gifts.

Brian also wanted a new bike, but his single mom didn't have two pennies to rub together, much less the money to buy him a new bicycle.

Brian's mother, Donna, started by truly listening to Brian's feelings about a new bike. She empathized with his desires, with no put-downs like "Why do you need a new bike when your old one is just fine?" or "How dare you ask for something so expensive when you know our money situation is so tight?"

She focused forward on solutions rather than the problem. "What could you do to get the bike you want?" She suggested they brainstorm some ideas. And she asked, "How can I support you in getting what you want?"

She listened again as he began to come up with some very creative ideas and gave him lots of love messages for his ingenuity and initiative. He sold some old skateboards and his old bike. He rounded up some odd jobs and got a few dollars more. He shopped furiously for bargains and the best value.

Donna refrained from ever "telling" Brian anything, but kept the questions coming when he started to get stuck. And throughout it all, she modeled good communication, good listening, problem solving, and more.

Both young people ended up with new bikes, but one got some invaluable life skills, and the other got a little bit more adept at manipulating other people. Tiffany knows how to get someone else to take care of her needs; Brian's self-esteem has soared knowing he can take care of himself. Which set of messages would you rather your children have?

How do we give our children this gift of abundance? As we've seen in the last story, each of the five tools helps foster this gift. What do we model to our children? Where do we focus? How often do we demonstrate what we can't do instead of what we can do? This tool didn't fix the leaky faucet? What else can I try? What are some other ways to solve the problem? Is it even a problem or maybe just another situation to tackle and learn from? Remember, our kids don't just mimic our words and actions, they also pick up on attitude.

How often are we asking questions instead of "telling"?

Even though we're the grown-ups and are supposed to know all the answers, I surely don't. This was especially true when we built that magnificent tree house. I hadn't ever really built much of anything before, but I didn't have to pretend to be big King Know-It-All to my girls. We simply operated out of that gift of abundance—there's always another way to do this, and the best way to find it is to ask questions.

When the girls wanted a bench over a certain branch, we explored the idea together. How big should it be? What direction did they want to face? What would make it strong enough for several people to sit on at once? How would it connect to the rest of the structure?

And, of course, it's so empowering to listen to all their ideas while constantly giving love messages to reinforce that there is always another time, another way, another day.

"You see things and you say 'Why?';
but I dream things that never were
and I say 'Why not?' "

—George Bernard Shaw

"Being responsible means knowing how to take care
of yourself. It means not asking silly questions
that you could figure out on your own.
But if you're hurt, be responsible
and go to an adult for help."

—Emily Vannoy, age 9

"Being responsible means you can stay by yourself
and your parents know you won't mess up.
They know you're trustworthy."

—Stefanie Fiser, age 9

"Honesty means don't tell lies.
It means people can trust you.
If you take someone else's gum and that person
asks you about it, you tell the truth even if you know
you could blame it on someone else
and no one would ever know.
When I don't tell the truth, my heart pounds
and it feels like it's covered up with water
and I'm drowning."

—Alison Vannoy, age 7

CHAPTER FOURTEEN

The Gifts of Integrity and Responsibility

Imagine a world where no one would ever be a victim again. Impossible, you say? There will always be war, famine, crime, poverty, disease, accidents—all sorts of terrible tragedies.

I absolutely agree; appalling things happen. None of us may be exempt from what seem to be crushing circumstances or events that are out of our control. Without the gifts of integrity and responsibility, however, we would become victims of almost any circumstance by giving away our power, by always blaming someone or something else.

Although I consider integrity and responsibility to be two separate gifts essential for my children to have, they also seem to be inseparable. When you accept personal responsibility, it seems only natural that integrity flows outward to encompass the world and its inhabitants as well.

With the gift of responsibility our children learn to take charge of their own lives; with the gift of integrity they learn to help others work through the circumstances they face.

With these qualities and values we take full responsibility for our circumstances and our future. We make intelligent decisions. We live our lives with pride, fairness, and dignity. Without integrity, our children don't trust themselves or anybody else. Worse yet, we don't know if we can trust our children.

Rachel remembered how to use all the tools in the new way when she had to deal with this situation.

> *My son was planning to go on a class outing to the zoo and wanted money for a souvenir. I told him to go to my purse, where there was a five-dollar bill and a ten-dollar bill, and take the five dollars. Later that day, I went out to lunch and was really embarrassed when I couldn't pay for it without borrowing money from my friend, because both bills were gone from my purse.*
>
> *I was ready to lambaste that kid. But I remembered the training and said to him, "I went to pay for my lunch today and didn't have any money. It was really embarrassing."*
>
> *He sheepishly admitted he took both and apologized. I realized I could have accused him of being a crook, but I chose instead to acknowledge him for telling the truth. He now has an image of himself as a high-integrity person and is scrupulously honest in all his dealings with me and others.*

Integrity, to me, is how you act when no one is watching, when no one knows what you're doing. It's always telling the truth, clearing up misconceptions or partial truths. It's never knowingly hurting anybody or anything. Parental integrity is not reading our children's mail or eavesdropping on their private conversations or snooping through their room. Integrity is keeping our commitments.

Integrity creates trust, and trust is a vital component of relationships. Would you want your best friend or your spouse to be someone you couldn't trust? Life without relationships is hollow, scary, lonely, lacking joy. In the corporate world, effective business leaders know tasks only get accomplished out of relationships; without them nothing gets done.

The gifts of integrity and responsibility are fundamental core qualities of our great teachers, spiritual advisers, business leaders, neighborhood activists, and indeed, great parents—whether you're working on a national scale or at home with your family.

> *In describing what the Fourth of July, Independence Day, meant to him, President Bill Clinton noted how he was raised by his grandparents and great-grandparents while his widowed mother attended nursing school. "None of us ever lacked for love or support," Clinton wrote. "The strength of our family could not be measured by the weight of our wallets.*
>
> *"That feeling of love and support may be the most valuable gift that a parent, a grandparent or a teacher can give to a child. It's a feeling that breeds responsible adults—citizens who, because they respect themselves, can respect others, can recognize the dignity of the lives and the work of their fellow citizens. And that is a glue for our communities." [Parade magazine, July 4, 1993]*

People like Martin Luther King, who helped people of all races recognize and respect the dignity of all human beings, exemplify the gifts of integrity and responsibility. And people like Mother Teresa, who selflessly looks after the poor and diseased that so many others would rather ignore. Like Jaime Escalante, the East Los Angeles mathematics teacher portrayed in the film *Stand and Deliver*, who turns unmotivated, discipline-problem students into scholastic superstars. Like Clarissa Pinkola Estés, who went from being a welfare mom to helping millions of men and women realize and celebrate the power, creativity, and courage of ordinary women through her work and her book *Women Who Run with the Wolves.* Like so many millions more unnamed and often unsung heroes who work quietly and diligently with AIDS patients or terminally ill children; who toil with homeless families or illiterate adults or troubled teenagers or mentally ill citizens or in crime-ridden neighborhoods. Like one parent or one teacher demonstrating a model of integrity and responsibility.

In each case, just one person is making a profound difference in someone else's life. Would you like your child to be such a person? How many of you think there is a general lack of integrity today—that people think they've done wrong only if they get caught? The issue is the same to me, whether it's a kid stealing candy from the corner grocery to powerful politicians or corporate leaders "stealing" from the public. Our society can only be as good as its individual members who maintain their own level of personal integrity.

Well, that's all pretty grandiose, you're probably thinking about now, but how do we deal with responsibility in our kids today at home where the important issues are about picking up their toys or keeping their room clean or doing their chores or remembering their lunch money?

When I was 16 and had just had my driver's license for a few months, someone crashed into me at a corner. I got a ticket—and a massive load of guilt worrying about how much trouble I'd be in. I lied to my papa about my fault in the accident. Whether or not he believed me, he let the issue ride.

Finally, I couldn't stand it any more. I woke him up at 11:00 one night to tell him what had really happened. I really admire his calm, almost terse way of handling the situation. He could have focused on how bad I was or how

terrible a driver I was, but instead he focused on my in-
tegrity in coming clean with him. He reminded me that
mistakes happen, but that I was a good person anyway. I re-
ally learned about working through painful situations from
that experience. His reaction endeared him to me and made
me realize integrity isn't about not getting caught. His
demonstration of unconditional acceptance gave me the
strength to develop integrity.

A mother told us at a "10 Greatest Gifts" seminar follow-up
session about the day she faced a similar situation. She was pan-
icked when she realized her 15-year-old, who had lost her driving permit because of several tickets, was out driving around
anyway. This mom fretted all day and worked herself into such
a frenzy she was ready to launch into her usual yelling tirade,
was prepared to lay on some pretty severe consequences when
her daughter made it home.

But she realized those were the methods she had always
used and her daughter was still displaying all sorts of irresponsible behavior. She decided instead to try all five parenting tools
in the new way.

"How did you feel about driving the car without a permit?"
she asked when the daughter got home. "What did you need
that you couldn't get some other way?" She listened to her
daughter with no blocks, no lectures, no "better ideas." She acknowledged the girl's feelings of being restricted, of wanting
grown-up freedom, wanting to be with her friends and not
liking to take the bus to the mall to meet them. Although the
girl's actions were not appropriate ways to act on those feelings,
this wise mom still acknowledged the presence of the feelings
and validated them.

She continued with questions, all of which continued focusing forward on what she was feeling, on what everyone could

"Integrity, to me, is how you act
when no one is watching,
when no one knows what you're doing.
It's always telling the truth,
clearing up misconceptions
or partial truths.
It's never knowingly hurting
anybody or anything."

"Integrity creates trust,
and trust is a vital component
of relationships."

"How many of you think there is a general lack
of integrity today—that people think they've
done wrong only if they get caught?
Our society can only be as good
as its individual members
who maintain their own level
of personal integrity."

learn from the incident, what solutions there were and how to move forward. There was no blame and no mention of how bad the girl was or how she had screwed up.

"What do you think would have happened if you'd been caught?" the mother asked. "How do you feel about the situation?" "What do you think we should do as your parents? What consequences do you think there should be? What are some other ways you could get what you need when you're feeling that way? How could we help you get what you need?"

This mom was ecstatic as she told the group about the incident.

> *All the telling and lecturing and punishment I used to get as a kid made me resent and hate my parents. All I did was think up new and creative ways to sneak out and do more of what they suspected I was doing anyway. Using the five tools and asking forward focus questions let my daughter take responsibility for the problem. She owned it, she learned from it, she came up with some very creative solutions.*
>
> *We weren't able to accept all the options she came up with, but at least we could discuss our limits with her without tearing into each other the way we used to do, leaving nothing but hurt and anger and escalating rebellion.*
>
> *She's been very responsible about using the car ever since she was able to reinstate her permit. Of course we acknowledge her responsibility every time she displays it, whether it's related to driving or not. I feel so much more comfortable now trusting her with the car—and with her life.*

"Old" parenting to me means we are taught *what* to think, not *how* to think. What's the cost of that kind of parenting? Can our children ever learn to be responsible that way? In all our work with schools, educators tell us over and over again how much they long for children who can think for themselves. Here's what one concerned teacher said.

*There's no way I can prepare children with what to think
about a future that is changing so rapidly. What are considered "facts" today will be challenged tomorrow. Lifelong
patterns their parents expected in the workplace and in society have disappeared. We can't even train the students for
a lifetime profession since the average person will make at
least seven different job or career transitions in their adult
years.*

*Children have to learn to live in more and more diverse
situations, with ever-broadening definitions of family and
sexuality and economic possibility and a variety of ethnic
mixes. My reality is not necessarily that child's reality or
that family's reality. I cannot teach your children or
my own what to think, but I can teach them how to learn
and explore and adapt and create—if they know how to
think and are willing to be responsible for themselves and
others.*

On one level, responsibility is about the environment and all
living things. Three-year-old Alexander loves to catch bugs and
toads and play with them, for example. His dad, Rick, gently reminds him not to play with them too much because the little
creatures might want to go home. As a result, Alexander's be-
coming very conservation oriented.

Integrity is about fairness. Allison recalls the time when she
and four-year-old Jason were visiting his grandmother. She and
her mother kept a running card game going over the week.
They kept score with pennies, and Allison recalls she was always soundly beaten by her mom. Jason always made it to the
kitchen first in the morning, however, and promptly evened out
the penny piles. "It was just the first of many ways he's demon-
strated a high degree of fairness and integrity in his life," Allison said.

Responsibility is also about consideration for other people.

My girls were sitting in the seat across from me on a train trip, playing and giggling between themselves. However, I noticed Emmy kept putting her feet up on the seat in front of her. I asked her to please not do that, it might be bothering the lady in front of her. But, of course, she kept doing it, allowing me to think for her and own her problem.

I was ready to escalate into some pretty heavy-handed power struggles with her. Yelling seemed like an option as well as physically removing her from that seat. But we all know by now how much good that would have done. Instead, I approached her from the new parenting paradigm.

"Emmy," I said, "I just realized I was doing your thinking for you. You know, about how you kept putting your feet up on the seat in front of you. I'm not going to do that anymore. You're in charge. What do you think would be the outcome of putting your feet up there? What do you think the people in the seats in front of you feel like with your feet up there? Why do you think it's good to put your feet up there? Why do you think it might not be a good idea to put your feet up there?"

Once she'd weighed the pros and cons of her own answers the problem disappeared. Her feet stayed on the floor while she went on enjoying the trip.

Once again the high road of parenting cultivated a whole different set of qualities and values.

Ten-year-old Sean has certain chores to do each week, including gathering together all the week's newspapers for recycling. He's a very responsible young man, but some "old" parenting messages have created so much resistance that his natural sense of responsibility is quickly fading.

What messages? Although he has never picked up the unread papers from their spot on the coffee table, his dad

" 'Old' parenting to me means we are taught
what to think, not how to think.
What's the cost of that kind of parenting?
Can our children ever learn to be responsible
that way?"

"The ability to make smart little choices
inevitably leads children to
trust themselves to make
more important choices
about the big issues in life, too."

"We all want to trust our kids,
but they have to trust us first."

"Instead of the usual 'trap and blame' questions
we're so accustomed to using,
we ask questions to help our children
accept responsibility and
work toward solutions."

constantly reminds him: "Don't forget when you put pa-
pers in the bag, don't take the ones on the coffee table—I
haven't read them yet."

"Why does he constantly tell me what to do before I even
do it?" Sean asks plaintively. "I don't mind doing my
chores, but I hate getting reminded about them all the time.
I know when I have to have them done, but I want to do
them my own way."

What are your reactions when a boss or your spouse or a
friend constantly nags you to do something you already know
you have to do? Much like Sean, I suspect the urge to resist and
retaliate becomes overwhelming, obliterating your own natural
sense of commitment and responsibility to do what needs to be
done. Not only do you resist like most children do, you probably start labeling yourself as irresponsible and move toward
that focus of irresponsibility.

A big part of the gift of responsibility, to me, is learning to
make wise choices. The ability to make smart *little* choices inevitably leads children to trust themselves to make more important choices about the big issues in life, too. Plus, imagine your
own peace of mind as you know and trust your children to
make the best possible life decisions for themselves.

I always feel sorry for the adults I know who still can't enjoy
a conversation with their parents. Take Mike, for instance.

I'm 35 years old and my parents still treat me like I am
five. They question everything I do. "Why are you still
working at that crummy job?" they'll say, or "Are you sure
that suit is the right color for you?" They'll ask me why my
wife is doing this or that and why I let my kids act like little
brats, or wouldn't we rather attend the church in the old
neighborhood?

I know they are really very good people and everything

*they did was to make me into a responsible adult, but how
can I feel responsible if they question every decision I make?
It's gotten so I hate to talk to them anymore, and we're finding more and more excuses not to visit. And it's really too
bad. My dad's health is declining and I'd like to enjoy more
of him during whatever time he has left rather than feel like
I want to avoid him.*

I saw my girls' sense of responsibility grow by leaps and
bounds recently. Their mom reminded me they needed some
new clothes for the summer.

*We went to the department store, where I promptly sat
down near the girls' department. They looked confused.
Wasn't I going to sort through everything, discard the stuff
I didn't like and then show them what they should buy? No,
I wasn't.*

*What I did was discuss with them how much money they
each had to spend. I asked them what size they wanted to
wear. They decided to get the clothes a little bit bigger than
they needed so the clothes would still fit in the fall.*

*I sat back and relaxed. They were delighted with the free-
dom to choose. I was delighted to see them compare items,
check for size and fit and price and suitability before making a choice. They left that store with armloads of clothes
they loved, never noticing the intangible gifts of responsibility and wise choices and self-esteem they'd gotten, too.*

*That evening a friend came over to spend the night with
them, and the three of them put on a delightful fashion
show, complete with music and commentary and even a little printed program.*

That incident led to another level of learning to live respon-
sibly a couple of days later.

After their friend had gone home, we were working on cleaning the house when we discovered a big stain on the carpet in their room. The friend had brought some makeup with her and had persuaded the girls to use it for the fashion show. Emmy and Ali thought they ought to use the makeup in the bathroom but their friend insisted they wouldn't spill it. It spilled anyway.

At first I was furious. Our landlady had installed beautiful new carpets and was very concerned that we take good care of them. One of my own measures of personal integrity is to leave a rented home in better shape than when I move in.

I was ready to hurl the whole old "king" dad routine at those little girls, making sure they knew how bad they were, and how irresponsible, how much of a burden they were, how I had to always follow them around and do their thinking for them. For good measure I'd call their friend's parents and let them know what an irresponsible little brat she was too.

Fortunately, Emmy and Ali remember the five tools faster than I do sometimes. They acknowledged the problem and wanted help finding a solution. They were not going to blame their friend; they had suggested using the bathroom but caved in to her idea not to. They knew they were going to stick to their own principles the next time someone tried to talk them into doing something they knew was wrong. They were willing to do whatever it took to get it cleaned up.

Questions, messages, focus, modeling, listening. We all used all the tools and the problem got handled. The rug looks terrific.

Modeling has to be one of the most important tools we can use to give our children the gifts of integrity and responsibility. My girls know, for example, that they can trust me with any kind of treasure. They'll often leave a pack of gum with me or candy or money and they know with absolute certainty that I will guard it with my life, no matter how trivial it might seem to me.

A young man who was at our house one day with his mom was getting pretty bored while the grown-ups were working. He noticed Emmy's Game Boy and wanted to play with it. The girls were visiting out of state and it would have been easy just to let him play with it. Instead, I said, "I'd love it if you could, but it's not mine. I have to clear it with the girls. Let's see if we can reach them and see what they say." We reached Emmy at her grandmother's and she said she'd love to let him play with it. They both learned a valuable lesson in integrity and responsibility.

Kids also need to know they can trust you with their secrets. It's so easy when parents get together to start swapping stories about silly or embarrassing things our kids have done. The adults just think they're cute anecdotes, but if the children were to hear us, they'd be mortified that we were exposing them to ridicule.

We all want to trust our kids, but they have to trust us first.

Very young children can't conceptualize honesty; until about the age of six or seven, they're still convinced they didn't do anything wrong if you didn't see them do it. But as we noted in the chapter about the Model Tool, they're learning every minute from your actions. We can't wait until their intellect finally matures enough to grasp the concept of honesty—they've already formed their definition of it from how you act when you think no one is looking.

The Listen Tool is crucial, too. Young children will often appear to be lying as they spin fanciful, elaborate tales. But in many instances, this is their truth, this is the way they see the world. Acknowledge their feelings, their creativity, and their talent for storytelling. It's a great time to use some forward focus questions to find out what the child likes best about this story, what happens next, or what some other outcomes might be.

The Teach Tool is essential. Instead of the usual "trap and blame" questions we're so accustomed to using, we ask questions to help our children accept responsibility and work toward solutions.

The old questions were ones like: What happened here? Who did this? Why did you do this? What's wrong with you? The new ones are: How do you feel about this? What are some other options to deal with this? What did you learn from this? Who else has been affected? What do we need to do to solve this? What do you think the consequences should be?

Using this new parenting paradigm, our focus, of course, is always on the forward side of the energy circle, and our messages reinforce and empower our children's acts of responsibility and integrity—and we can discard some more bricks out of the parenting backpack.

> We love to take long walks in the woods around our new mountain home. The first time my girls and I took a walk there was during a very rainy week. We got back with muddy shoes and soggy clothes. Before we even rounded the corner to our driveway, I mentally started my list of instructions on what they should do. "Take off your shoes before you go in the house. Put your socks in the washer, hang your jackets in the right place so they can drip."
>
> Uh-oh, I thought, if I start thinking for them now, I might as well count on doing it for the rest of their lives. Instead I asked, "How should we deal with coming back into the house when we're all dirty like this?" No surprise: they came up with the same suggestions I'd been ready to order them to do, and they even thought of a few more things like cleaning off the dog's tummy as well as his paws so he wouldn't leave dirt when he lay down. I'd swear the girls

*looked two inches taller knowing that I respected and hon-
ored their ideas. And I haven't had to be concerned about
the problem since.*

They are very responsible young girls.

"The best portion of a good man's life
is his little, nameless, unremembered
acts of kindness and of love."

—William Wordsworth

"Every action of our lives touches
on some chord that will vibrate
in eternity."

—Edwin Hubbel Chapin

"I like it when people make decisions
based on what they want and think,
and not on what other people say."

—Lindy Kedro, age 13

"I like it when I make an important decision
and it turns out to be a good choice for me."

—Casey Lebsack, age 14

CHAPTER FIFTEEN

The Gift of Conscious Choice

Conscious choice is the most empowering resource that I have in my life. I can't control what happens in the world, but I can certainly control how I respond to whatever does happen.

I remember as I was growing up back on the farm that I didn't want to be like the steers with such narrow lives: We confined them to a little pen, led them around by the ring in their nose, fattened them up and then took them to the slaughterhouse.

To me, the gift of conscious choice means taking the ring out of my nose. It means not operating "on automatic," not always reacting out of the back side of the energy circle instead of acting proactively from the forward side.

A number of recent studies confirm that the most stressed-out workers are those who feel they have no control over the circumstances around them. Many people have tightly constricted circumstances in their jobs, but I have seen two people

"To me, the gift of conscious choice
means not operating 'on automatic,' not
always reacting out of the back side
of the energy circle instead of
acting proactively
from the forward side."

"The only variable link between an event
and its outcome is your reaction.
That's the key to conscious choice
— your reaction."

"Once you know that you have the gift of choice
in your life, there is no more powerful tool.
It allows you to figure out
how to make things happen
and how not to be a victim,
no matter what the circumstances."

in identical windowless office cubicles or on the same fast-paced production line react completely differently to those same circumstances.

Remember that equation I talked about earlier that showed the only variable link between an event and its outcome is your reaction? That's the key to conscious choice—your reaction.

Here's what happened to me in what was a thoroughly bleak situation, until my mother gave me the gift of conscious choice.

My daughters and I had planned a magnificent old-fashioned country Christmas. We would enjoy an exciting train ride to my parents' farm in Nebraska where we would celebrate a perfect holiday with homemade cookies, a tree we would cut out in the pasture, presents, and warm loving grandparents.

A phone call from Ma a week before Christmas shattered that dream with the announcement that Pa was ill with gall-bladder problems. Worse yet, the doctor had also found a tumor on his kidney. Surgery was scheduled for two days before Christmas. They wanted me to come, but I'd have to leave the kids behind.

What a disappointment! It was the first Christmas I was going to be able to spend with my daughters since the divorce. And even worse, my Pa might be dying. The train ride back was cold and lonely, the worst I ever had. It was the first time I had ever faced losing one of my parents and the past two years had been so full of loss. I was drained physically and emotionally.

The weather was frigid and dreary. As I sat on the cold stiffness of a hospital chair at my father's side on Christmas Eve, I mourned the possibility of losing him. Despair wrapped me in a thick blanket of self-pity and anger that my holiday was ruined. I couldn't believe how little hope

*life had at that moment. I'd lost all my old dreams and
didn't have any new ones.*

*Another phone call was my salvation. I'd sent Ma home
to rest. I called to comfort her, I rationalized, but the minute
she answered, I realized how much I needed her.*

*She spoke with a strong positive radiance. Merry
Christmas to me. And wasn't it wonderful Pa had the gall-
bladder problem so that all the testing had uncovered the
kidney problem when it could still be fixed? Because he'd
been sick, so many people had called that she might never
have heard from. And here I was home for Christmas. She
had beautiful grandchildren. Even if Pa didn't make it for
some reason, she'd had a wonderful life with him. Her
warmth and joy punctuated the call.*

*I stared at the phone. Were Ma and I in the same reality?
How could she be so up when I was so down? We had the
same package of facts, but she was elated while I was scared
to death.*

*And then the light of realization dawned. We were shar-
ing the same experience but only our attitude made it a positive or negative reality. What if I could pass that positive
focus and gift of conscious choice on to my young girls?
What a difference that could make in their lives! Because of
her attitude, the rest of that evening and the entire week
would become a celebration.*

Once you know that you have the gift of choice in your life,
there is no more powerful tool. It allows you to figure out how
to make things happen and how not to be a victim, no matter
what the circumstances. Just listen to how two neighbors
who've experienced the same hurricane or flood or other apparently tragic situation react to the devastation around them. They
both may have lost all their possessions, their home, their personal treasures, but even in the midst of their intense grief, one

will view it as the end of the world while the other will see it as the beginning of a new opportunity. Which way would you rather have your children react?

I remember a teacher who had participated in one of our leadership seminars. She was extraordinarily quiet throughout the sessions and her colleagues pointed out to me how her aura of doom and gloom affected the whole school.

But on the fourth day she burst out of her shell. "Something tragic happened to me a few years ago and I believed I had no reason to live since then. I haven't engaged in life at all. I just show up when and where I'm supposed to be. After learning about conscious choice and how I can focus on what I want instead of all my problems and why I'm such a poor victim, for the first time in four years, I'm excited about living again!"

Learning about choices can start on the most basic level. While we were having breakfast one morning, I asked my girls, "What do you want to do today?" I asked what they wanted to accomplish around the house because I knew they were working on a couple of projects.

"What do you think is the best way to accomplish these things?" I continued. I asked if they wanted to help me with a couple of projects, letting every answer be their choice.

They stayed busy all day long and I scarcely even knew they were around. What a difference from the days when I was doing their thinking for them instead of letting them make their own choices. What an obvious difference I could see in their pride, self-esteem, and their sense of responsibility.

Can you spot all the parenting tools—focus, model, listen, questions, and messages—in this situation I faced recently?

I had an important business lunch to attend. I asked the girls: "Would you rather go to a neighbor's house or come with me to the restaurant?" They wanted to come with me. "How could we both enjoy our time there, remembering

*that I have to concentrate on my work with the client?"
They would sit at a table across the room and have their
own lunch meeting. "If you come along to a nice restaurant, what kind of behavior would be appropriate at that
kind of place?" They described perfectly behaved young
people. "When you look at the menu, what do you think
would be the best thing to order? You know, it's completely
your choice what to have."*

*"We'll look at the prices first," they said, "and we'll make
sure it's something we like to eat so we'll finish our plates."*

*The meeting went off without a hitch. But far more im-
portant to me was seeing how many good choices those little girls made, and how they followed through on what they
chose because they were their own choices. I could have told
them and told them how to behave and what to order and
not to bother me while I was working—and I know I
wouldn't have been able to concentrate on a word my client
said, wondering at what moment they would start misbehaving. How else could they react when the messages I
would have sent were ones like "I've got to think for you. I
can't trust you to behave in public. You're not able to
choose what you want to eat or how to act. I know you're
going to bother me."*

*Instead the messages they got were exactly the opposite. I
have no hesitation about trusting them completely as they
grapple with harder decisions and situations as they grow
into adulthood.*

A friend related to me the tragic consequences of backward
focus messages in her family and how she discovered the gift of
conscious choice on her own.

*My dad was a typical "I'll tell you what to think and
when to think it" kind of parent. As an adult, I ended up*

drinking too much to ease the pain of not being a "real" person. But I also made the conscious choice to get sober and break those old patterns in my own family.

But a painful choice I've had to make is to restrict my children's contact with their grandfather. It's such a shame because everyone loses. He doesn't get to experience what terrific grandsons he has, and they miss the opportunities I think kids should have with a grandparent.

I lent my copy of the "10 Greatest Gifts" audiotape to my mother because she's much more open to using the tools and that's the way I want others to treat my children. Unfortunately my dad's still stuck on the back side of the energy circle. He expects my two preschoolers to sit still through a two- or even three-hour family dinner, all the while pointing out how poorly behaved they are and how bad they are—focusing on all the problems and "spots" he can.

When they do misbehave (by his definition, of course—and what else would they do since we go toward what we're focused on as well as being unable to avoid a don't), he's still convinced that physically disciplining them is the only way they'll learn respect. I know what they're really learning is that if you're bigger you get the power, that hurting someone is OK, that they're bad kids, that they can't think for themselves, and that they aren't supposed to feel their own feelings.

On top of it all, my sister, who's in her 30s, is still reacting to all those old messages we grew up with. She wonders why her life is so aimless and why she can't commit to a relationship with a wonderful man who loves her deeply. I know it's because he's not someone my parents approve of, and they're forcing her to choose between him and them.

She hasn't figured out yet that they've been thinking for her all her life. They've chosen her clothes, her friends, her jobs, her places to live. But even when she goes along with

"I used to leave business meetings
beating myself up for everything
that went wrong. By the time
I pulled out of the parking lot
I knew exactly who to blame for whatever I felt
had gone wrong or had convinced myself
I was a complete idiot for what I had said
or done wrong. As I left a meeting one day,
after having decided to practice
conscious choice more often,
I immediately made a choice to focus
on what went well in that meeting.
I thought about what my bosses had liked
about what I said and what I could do
to move my part of the project forward.
What a difference!
Instead of moping, I was energized.
My sense of responsibility soared.
My energy on the job the next day
was ten times what it usually was."

*all their choices, they still focus on her spots. She can never
do it right. She can never win at life.*

Fortunately, we don't have to wait until things get that
awful to learn to use conscious choice. I find myself stopping in
my tracks dozens of times a day, remembering that I can choose
the way I want to react to a situation.

I used to leave business meetings beating myself up for
everything that went wrong. By the time I pulled out of the
parking lot I knew exactly who to blame for whatever I felt had
gone wrong or had convinced myself I was a complete idiot for
what I had said or done wrong.

As I left a meeting one day, after having decided to practice
conscious choice more often, I immediately made a choice to
focus on what went well in that meeting. I thought about what
my bosses had liked about what I said and what I could do to
move my part of the project forward.

What a difference! Instead of moping all the way home, I
was energized. My confidence mounted as I patted myself on
the back for what I had done right. My sense of responsibility
soared. My energy on the job the next day was ten times what it
usually was.

It works well in my family too.

*My girls and I arrived home from a recent trip with a
terribly dirty car. I had reminded them that I really liked the
way they were taking responsibility for both our new house
and the new car. I had said, "You've been so careful on this
trip. How would you feel when we get home if we clean up
the car before we go exploring in our enchanted forest?" As
we stood in the driveway washing the car, I noticed some
spots they had missed. Just as I was ready to point them out
I noticed one of those critical junctures in my life where I
can either lapse back into old, low-road parenting or choose*

to take the high road. I realized it was just as easy to notice the places they'd done well as the places they'd missed.

It would have immediately taken the fun out of an otherwise enjoyable chore if I had harped on the places they had missed. The girls would have wanted to quit right then or at least they'd have grumbled about how no one appreciated them after they'd tried so hard. I'm sure you know the standard responses. Who wants to help a parent again who's constantly criticizing the job they're doing?

When I acknowledged them for the remarkable job they'd done on the mirrors or the left bumper, for example, I could see their focus shift immediately. On their own they went back to the places that were less than perfect and worked their hearts out to make them as spotless as the rest of the car.

I know you've already encountered many times when conscious choice made an incredible difference in your life and you found that you don't have to go through life as a helpless victim of circumstance. As you continue on this path, FAC yourself for modeling and giving such a valuable gift to your children.

"The last of the human freedoms—
to choose one's attitude
in any given set of circumstances,
to choose one's own way."

—Viktor Frankl

CHAPTER SIXTEEN

Recipe for Partnership

I was only ten years old, but I already knew enough about Nebraska weather and pests to be worried about our neighbor, Max. He'd just suffered a serious back injury and this was wheat harvest time. I knew that the grain had to be harvested the minute it was ripe—otherwise there was a frightening chance the crop would be lost to wind, rain, hail, grasshoppers, or some other disaster.

I hadn't noticed any neighbors even dropping by to see how Max was doing—that is, not until the first day the wheat was ripe. I looked out across the section that morning and there were six combines, extra trucks, farmers, hired men, and farm wives with plenty of food, swarming over Max's wheat fields.

These thoughtful neighbors didn't wait to be asked for help. And they didn't ask Max if he needed help, because he probably would have said no. They simply pitched right in to harvest his fields, even before they combined their own wheat.

"The one factor that enhances the learning
environment and student achievement
is parental involvement—not meddling,
not blaming, not criticizing, but sincere,
helpful involvement."

"Except for the relationship with our children,
I think that our relationships with their
care providers and teachers are the most
important alliances we'll ever have."

"Our society simply can't afford to fix any
more broken adults. It's so much easier and
cost-effective to build a healthy child."

Back in those days, that same community watched over me, too. Everyone—neighbors, local shopkeepers, the grain elevator manager, teachers, the pastor—all formed an extended family who loved me and showed as much concern for my well-being as my own nuclear family did.

In thinking about family partnerships, I'm also reminded of an old story about two brothers who farmed side by side.

> *A long time ago, two brothers shared a grain field and a mill. After toiling together each day, they would divide the grain equally between them.*
>
> *One day, the first brother, who had no family, thought to himself, "This isn't fair! I don't have anybody and my brother has a large family to feed." So each night, after dark, he took an extra portion of grain over to his brother's bin—and nobody ever knew it.*
>
> *Not long after that, the second brother said to himself, "This isn't fair! My brother doesn't have anybody and I have sons who will grow up to take care of me." So every night after dark he took part of his grain over to his brother's bin—and nobody ever knew it.*
>
> *But one night they met unexpectedly on the path and learned what each had been doing. They wept with joy at the depth of their love and dedication for each other.*

Each of these stories represents to me an outstanding model of family and community love and commitment. It's sad that we seem to have lost this sense of responsibility and partnership in today's society. At a number of recent "10 Greatest Gifts" sessions, I've asked participants what the cost of this loss is to our youth. Their answers are the same across the country: kids growing up without guidance, a lack of bonding between children and an adult, lowered self-esteem, school dropouts, and increased drug use, crime, violence, and teenage pregnancy.

Unlike the community that worked in partnership for me as a child, I see various groups today almost at war over our children.

Frustrated parents complain about the high price of child care, rapid turnover in staff or providers' lack of skills. They want more personal attention for their child. They criticize teachers, the cost of bloated school bureaucracies, irrelevant studies, and violence in schools.

At the same time, child care providers and teachers are frustrated with the lack of parent interest and parent involvement. Care providers frequently tell me how amazed they are to get a call at night from parents who are desperate for someone to watch their child the next day, but who have not checked out the facilities or discussed their child-rearing philosophies and practices.

"We're neither respected nor appreciated by parents," Cynthia lamented. "Parents seem to think we're just another babysitter. I know life is hectic and stressful for today's parents, but I despair at how often they choose a child care facility for its cheaper price or more convenient location rather than the quality of care."

Research over the past 25 years has consistently shown that the one factor that enhances the learning environment and student achievement is parental involvement—not meddling, not blaming, not criticizing, but sincere, helpful involvement.

Yet teachers complain that no one comes to parents' night at school. "On one hand, they want us to teach their children everything they don't have time or don't want to teach at home, and then complain that we're teaching their kids things that oppose their family values," is a typical complaint I hear from educators. "Or parents criticize us for being paid too much for too little work, or say that society's problems are a direct result of what our schools are or aren't doing. It's a constant struggle. We can't win."

Except for the relationship with our children, I think that our relationships with their care providers and teachers are the most important alliances we'll ever have. I'm sure you're aware that in many other societies, people who take care of children are the most highly esteemed people in the community. These cultures know that the hand that rocks the cradle indeed rules the world because caretakers and teachers wield so much influence in our children's formative years.

Research shows that many of our kids spend up to 75 percent of their waking time with someone other than their parents. An increasing number of children are entering full-time child care as early as six weeks of age. And, since most professionals believe children obtain at least 40 percent of their intellectual and personal development by age four, parents are understandably concerned that they are doing something more than simply parking or warehousing their children during all those hours.

Study after study shows how important quality early education is for children. One analysis, The High/Scope Perry Preschool Study, has followed a control group of students to age 27. The results are astonishing. A few thousand dollars invested in these kids for preschool education has resulted in significantly higher monthly earnings at age 27 for both men and women; significantly higher percentages of home ownership; higher levels of schooling completed; a significantly lower percentage receiving social services at some time in the previous ten years; and fewer arrests by age 27, including significantly fewer arrests for crimes of drug making or dealing.

Bottom line, our society simply can't afford to fix any more broken adults. The cost of Band-Aids is just too prohibitive and they don't work anyway. Compare these factors: It costs about $30,000 per person for a year in prison, or $50,000 per child in the juvenile justice system. On the other hand, it costs only about $2000 a year for a good preschool experience. It's so much easier and cost-effective to build a healthy child.

So, if we know all this, why are we still at war with each other?

I was listening to a nationally broadcast psychologist on the radio recently. A caller was distraught that her child's care provider allowed her son to watch Sesame Street longer than the half-hour limit this mother imposed on TV watching, and she was upset that her son was getting what she considered nonnutritious snacks. The longer the mother talked, the angrier she got.

When the psychologist finally interrupted to ask why she stayed with this care provider, the mother replied, "Because, except for these two things, there's a hundred reasons why she's terrific." What a classic case of not being able to see a whole lot of beauty because of a couple of spots!

Parents don't care. Teachers don't teach. Child care providers are devalued. I'd like to propose a new vision for an alliance between the significant adults in our children's lives. Imagine what it would be like if families, teachers, administrators, care providers, counselors, coaches—all our children's "educarers"—teamed up to create a new model of community, a new partnership to enhance our children's growth and development. Can you think of any group in America that could make a more profound and vital difference than such a partnership—working together at the core level of creating healthy communities and citizens and future workers? I'm convinced such a group could have more impact in one month than government could have in an entire year.

It's not that we haven't tried partnership before, but the old methods didn't work. Progressive leaders have always known that cooperation is critical to our children's development. But the old ways we tried to "work" together seemed to focus on blaming each other, pointing out our differences and "telling" each other how things ought to be done—or just giving up. The only way I've found to create genuine partnership is to use forward focus questions which concentrate on what's working, where we want to go, and how to achieve the results we want.

Parents and educators who have begun using the five tools along with the following "Recipe for Partnership" have reported exciting results in their homes and classrooms. "These forward focus questions have turned not only parent-teacher conferences, but every conversation I have with a parent, into a productive experience instead of a nightmare," said one Colorado teacher.

These forward-thinking partners have started to rebuild that important community we've been missing for so many years.

THE 10 GREATEST GIFTS
RECIPE FOR PARTNERSHIP
to create community, partnership, and cooperation between parents, teachers, and care providers.

Preparation That Helps Create Partnership:
• What kind of difference would it make if educators, care providers, and parents could create a unique bond or partnership concerning the children they mutually care for and care about?
• What kind of difference would it make if educators, care providers, and parents could present a unified approach to working with children?

Ingredients That Help Create Partnership:
• What are the aspects you are most pleased with

that are creating value for your child at our school or center? What do you think is causing those successes?

• What outcomes are most important for your children; what should they learn here? How will that benefit your child, family, and the school?

• What are some things we can both do to create even greater value for the children?

Tools That Help Create Partnership:
• Focus forward on what's working and where you want to be.
• Give caring, validating messages to your students, their parents—everyone.
• Teach by asking forward focus questions.
• Listen to your students and their parents.
• Model the qualities that support the growth of healthy, joyful individuals.

Mix Together Your Actions + Parents' Support to Achieve:
• Children who are secure in their self-esteem, who are learning to be responsible, self-confident, honest, and considerate; children who are educable.
• Parents who are secure in knowing that their vision for their children is understood and practiced by educators and care providers.
• Educators and care providers who are working with both the parent and child, knowing what qualities and values are important to the parent, and modeling them.

At the End of Every Day, Ask Yourself:
• What did I do today that I am most pleased about that helped my students? That helped their parents?

- How will that benefit them?
- What can I do tomorrow to help my students and their parents even more?

···

Although I've heard hundreds of stories from parents, teachers, and care providers about how using this "recipe" has helped reverse disintegrating relationships, saved lost business, and even staved off potential lawsuits, let me close with just one rewarding story Jamie, a child-care provider, shared. How little it can cost to save even one potentially "lost" child!

I'd had Justin in my care for four years, since he was just five months old. But his behavior problems started getting so out of hand I was actually considering terminating the relationship. What a loss that would have been to all of us! There was no way I wanted to break the bond Justin and I shared, as well as the friendships he had developed with the other children. Four-and-a-half-year-old children have so many more important things to deal with in their lives than the pain of a disruption in their other "family."

Unfortunately, my relationship with his parents had deteriorated over the past months. I blamed them for not telling me about problems they were having at home which could give me some clues about how to deal with Justin. They accused me of being stressed out because of some of my own personal issues and taking it out on their child. I almost didn't want to talk to them anymore because our conversations went nowhere.

I decided to use this unique 10 Greatest Gifts "recipe" at a parent potluck. We used forward focus questions and all five tools to discuss ways to relieve stress levels for everyone. The results were phenomenal! I felt valued, all the fam-

ilies felt involved and Justin's behavior problems were no longer any big deal. Most important, he was able to stay with the same loving, consistent caregiver. And what a pleasure for all of us to share a special place in our hearts for each other!

A few months after sharing this story, Jamie added this delightful postscript.

Our partnership/relationship was even more powerful than I realized. Justin's mom remarried a few months ago and was able to resign from her job and stay at home. But even though she no longer needs child care for Justin, she still brings him here several days a week because she feels our relationship is so important for both her child and her family. All our lives are enriched—and it all could have been so easily lost.

It takes an entire village to raise a child.

—African proverb

Solutions, Please

An old man was walking along the beach one day as the tide was going out. He moved slowly down the shoreline, picking up starfish that had been stranded on the shore and throwing them back in the water. A young man came along and watched the old man as he progressed down the beach saving starfish after starfish. "You must be crazy if you think you can help all the starfish," the young fellow said, staring at him in disbelief. "Do you know how long this shore is and how many starfish there are?"

The old man listened thoughtfully as the young man ranted. "I know this is a long shore and there are a lot of starfish," he replied. "But I can make a difference with this one starfish," he said as he threw another one into the water. "And I can make a difference with this one . . . and this one . . . and this one."

During the weeks I was finishing up this book, wherever I turned I was constantly reminded of the endless vista stretching before our society well into the next century. Unfortunately, it is a scene full of crime and violence, guns and gangs, dysfunctional or abusive families, schools that don't work, kids who won't learn, parents who can't love.

At least that's the "shoreline" of crises and problems that the critics see. But I see ways each and every parent, grandparent, teacher, or spiritual or corporate or social leader can truly make a difference—one child at a time, one family, one classroom, one office, one neighborhood at a time.

I was very touched by a mother at a recent "10 Greatest Gifts" session who reminded us all day long of how mad she was at her husband because he didn't attend the session. She knew her husband never came to any kind of classes, especially one about parenting, which people are somehow supposed to know instinctively how to do.

Instead of staying mad, this thoughtful mom decided to be responsible herself. No matter what her husband did or didn't do, she knew she could start using the five tools the new way with her children. She could start seeing his beauty instead of his spots. She could do it "one starfish at a time."

On a societal level, however, I realize our problems often appear too immense to confront. They seem so huge and so entrenched, we can't even figure out where to open the first door, much less how to devise a meaningful and lasting solution. Remember that wonderful saying, "Let there be peace on earth and let it begin with me"? Society's problems are not some amorphous blob of mindless, faceless "things" that can be "fixed." Each perpetrator of a crime, every person with a hand on a weapon, every participant in a disturbance is a human being with a heart, a mind, and a soul.

Where else to start but with our families, where each one of those human beings must begin? Whether it's a nuclear family, an extended family, a foster family or any other combination of caring human beings, we must start somewhere. And although it takes considerable energy and commitment, changing a family is certainly easier than changing a corporation or a neighborhood or any other large organization.

And as we change the culture of our families, surely the change will radiate out to affect those around us. If we touch just one child or one spouse or one neighbor or one co-worker, each of those will touch another three or five people, who will touch even more in an ever-radiating circle of change.

This reminds me of a fable I've heard many versions of over the years which offers a powerful example of a circle of change.

A great order of monks had gradually diminished over the years until there were only five brothers left living in what had once been a thriving monastery. People from all over the community had once come to the monastery for learning and spiritual renewal. Now, no one ever visited as the spirit of the place and its inhabitants seemed to be slowly dying.

One day, however, a rabbi happened by to visit. As he was leaving, Brother Timothy asked the rabbi if he could give them some advice on how to revitalize their dying order and make it an important spiritual center once again.

The rabbi said he was sorry, he had no advice to give them. "The only thing I can tell you," he said, "is that the Messiah is one of you."

The brothers were flabbergasted. The Messiah among them? Impossible!

They puzzled over this revelation for weeks. If the Messiah were here, which one could it be? Maybe it was the Abbot, Timothy. He had been the leader for years and would surely be chosen to be the Messiah.

"I see ways each and every parent, grandparent,
teacher, or spiritual or corporate or social leader
can truly make a difference—one child at a time,
one family, one classroom, one office,
one neighborhood at a time."

"Society's problems are not some amorphous blob
of mindless, faceless 'things' that can be 'fixed.'
Each perpetrator of a crime, every person with
a hand on a weapon, every participant
in a disturbance is a human being
with a heart, a mind, and a soul.
Where else to start but with our families,
where each one of those human beings
must begin?"

"If we're always focusing on the problem,
charging in to correct it, putting out fires,
telling people how they should be
or what they shouldn't have done,
we'll simply get more of the same.
We'll always be a fireman or a cop
or, sadly, an undertaker."

It couldn't be Brother Mark. He was always so argumen-
tative, but he was usually right. Perhaps he was the Mes-
siah? No, it was probably Brother Pius. He was so quiet as
he went about his work tending the garden and the animals.
He could probably nourish a troubled world as well as he
did his flocks if he were the Messiah.

But then, surely it would be Brother Dominick. He was
so studious, so learned. He knew all the great spiritual
writings of history, so it must be him. It couldn't be Peter,
could it? The Messiah certainly couldn't be the one who
was so ordinary, the one who cleaned toilets and dirty laun-
dry and scrubbed the pots and pans each day. Or could it?

Since the monks couldn't figure out which one of them
was the Messiah, they began to treat each other as though
each were the one. And just in case he himself might be the
one, each monk began to treat himself with new respect and
dignity.

In just a few weeks, the occasional visitors who did drop
by were awed by the love and goodness and new conscious-
ness at the monastery. They came back over and over again
and brought new friends along. Soon a few young men
asked if they could join such an outstanding order. The
monastery thrived again.

One monk at a time . . . one starfish . . . one child . . . one
family.

I want to leave you with an equally powerful message of
hope. Certainly, we've got big problems, but if we keep focusing
on symptoms, or putting on Band-Aids and applying other
short-term solutions, we only get short-term results. That's not
only discouraging, it's also disempowering to keep hearing
how bad everything is, especially when we know we go toward
what we focus on.

But if we get to the core, the roots of people's motivation

"We can't tell people how to be responsible or trustworthy or how to make good decisions. We can only create and nurture an environment and culture that allow those qualities to flourish."

"I have a firm belief that the cycle of functional families is just as transgenerational as the cycle of dysfunctional families. I believe deep down that the vast majority of people—whether children or adults—would rather make a difference in this world. We must create the environment that will nurture these qualities and values instead of destroy them."

"Every cell in our body has the potential to hurt or heal. Every interaction in every relationship has the same capability."

"What would happen if we did nothing else but celebrate the family, really concentrating on and appreciating what we have and what's good about each other?"

and their "want to," their personal responsibility and trustworthiness, their self-esteem, their true caring for the planet and other human beings, we don't need Band-Aids or more laws.

In the corporate world, billions of dollars are spent on TQM training, negotiation skills, conflict resolution skills, and team building training. Corporate leaders continually tell us that this skill-based training alone doesn't do much good if the employees don't come to the job with their own internal core values. Enlightened organizations can do a great deal to nurture those core values, and so can our schools. But how much further could these groups take everyone if they got more of them at home?

What happens if we hear an extremely "hot" motivational speaker who gets the audience bouncing off the ceiling with enthusiasm but fails to help the audience internalize the material? How soon does all that enthusiasm wear off? How soon do we forget all that information? How many more billions of dollars will be wasted trying to fix the problem?

Just as in the corporate world, there is no quick fix for our families. Band-Aids don't work. If we're always focusing on the problem, charging in to correct it, putting out fires, telling people how they should be or what they shouldn't have done, we'll simply get more of the same. We'll always be a fireman or a cop or, sadly, an undertaker.

The American dream for generation after generation is to make the world a better place for our children and our grandchildren. Those who measure that dream by finances and cars and careers and bigger houses have started to give up, realizing that aspiration isn't always possible.

But those who are measuring their dream by the true "gifts" they give their children have found their promise can be fulfilled. We can all give our children the qualities and values and principles that will shape their lives for the better while greatly influencing future generations and society as a whole.

It still amazes me, though, how many parents say it can't be done. They'll swear to it as they mutter about how crazy we are to even consider this kind of approach with children. Ask them questions? Listen to them without telling them how their idea won't work or what a better idea we have? Pay attention to our own behavior realizing that they'll do what we do, not what we say? Stay focused on what they're doing right instead of what they're doing wrong? Sheer madness, they tell us.

Many of these parents are considered model parents. They care deeply about their families. They try hard to do what they've been taught is the right thing. They are totally involved with the schools and their communities. They put lots of time and attention into their children's activities.

But overall, they're doing the same old thing they've always done, thinking they're doing everything possible. Not only are the old techniques not working, they are actually reinforcing the problems. These parents continue to focus on problems, on the other family members' spots, constantly telling everyone what to do, when to do it, and how to do it.

That approach goes against basic human nature. We can't tell people how to be responsible or trustworthy or how to make good decisions. We can only create and nurture an environment and culture that allow those qualities to flourish.

I wonder what would happen to all the abuse in the world if we focused on what was good about each other instead of what was bad? I never physically abused my daughters, but I certainly subjected them to some verbal and mental abuse. I was always attacking them: Why didn't they know better, why didn't they think first, what was wrong with them? I kept focusing on how they weren't perfect. Looking back, I think this was as harmful as any form of physical abuse could be.

So many parents have called after "10 Greatest Gifts" sessions and told us how dramatically abuse—including the subtle put-downs, sarcasm, and teasing—has declined in their family.

They've found it is possible to make a profound shift into a functional, joyful family.

I have a firm belief that the cycle of functional families is just as transgenerational as the cycle of dysfunctional families.

I believe deep down that the vast majority of people— whether children or adults—would rather make a difference in this world. They would rather be trustworthy, committed, and responsible, using their creativity and being joyful. But when we look at the average person, he or she is in the exact opposite position. We must create the environment that will nurture these qualities and values instead of destroy them.

Every cell in our body has the potential to hurt or heal. Every interaction in every relationship has the same capability. Every interaction can either hurt or heal; we can just get the job done, or we can get the job done while nurturing priceless qualities and values.

Which way do you want to go? What environment would you like for your family? How would that environment affect creativity, joy, productivity, the qualities and values your children receive, your peace of mind, your time for relaxation? Whose job is it to create that environment?

What would happen if we did nothing else but celebrate the family, really concentrating on and appreciating what we have and what's good about each other? Can you imagine what would happen? Our families would always be going forward, self-esteem would soar, trust and communication and joy would skyrocket. We would be building an incredible future for ourselves, our children, and our grandchildren.

Remember the two moms in the grocery store approaching their children from completely different frameworks of parenting—one scolded her child for touching the apples, the other praised her child for her curiosity about the broccoli? Here are two other children's equally opposite approaches to life.

> *A church picnic was being held in a beautiful city park just as all the roses were blooming. Two little girls had run back from inspecting a gorgeous rose bush to share their experience with their mothers.*
>
> *The first one rushed up to her mom and said: "Mommy, all the roses have thorns on them."*
>
> *The other one said: "Mommy, all the thorns have roses on them."*

Which is your approach to life? Which attitude would you prefer your children have? Where will they learn one or the other?

I'd like to close with this anonymous piece I keep near me at all times as a reminder of the power of unconditional love—with our families and the entire world.

People are sometimes unreasonable, illogical, and self-centered. Love them anyway.
If you do good, people may accuse you of selfish motives. Do good anyway.
If you are successful, you may win false friends and true enemies. Succeed anyway.
The good you do today may be forgotten tomorrow. Do good anyway.
Honesty and transparency make you vulnerable. Be honest and transparent anyway.
What you spend years building may be destroyed overnight. Build anyway.
People who really want help may attack you if you help them. Help them anyway.
Give the world the best you have and you may get hurt. Give the world your best anyway.
The world is full of conflict. Choose peace of mind anyway.

—Anonymous

"It's a funny thing about life; if you refuse to accept anything but the best, you very often get it."

—Somerset Maugham

The 10 Greatest Gifts Project

We all have outstanding dreams and visions about what our families would be like when our children were born or adopted or blended into our family. But all too quickly the demands of modern life begin to chip away at our vision with the perpetual demands and problems of schedules, jobs, finances, and the endless to-do list of daily activity.

Parents who have attended our sessions say: *"This has turned our family from crisis to joy"; "This has brought me back to the joy of parenting"; "I just never realized how proactive I could be in giving my children the really important things—the qualities and values that develop internal commitment and responsibility."*

The 10 Greatest Gifts project provides keynote addresses, workshops, seminars, articles, research, organizational assistance, and newsletters dedicated to helping families get back in touch with their dream—what they really want from their family and how to get it. For more information regarding The 10 Greatest Gifts project-facilitator certification, or for information about audio and video tapes or other materials, please call 800-569-1877 or write to: The 10 Greatest Gifts Project, P.O. Box 1140, Morrison, CO 80465.

From all of us at the Vannoy Group,
thanks for caring enough to give the gifts
of internal qualities and values to your children, students,
grandchildren, and all the children of the world.